From
BREAKDOWN
To
Breakthrough

SHEYNA L. HEARD

From
BREAKDOWN
To
Breakthrough

Keys to Obtaining
Victory in Adversity

ROHI PUBLISHING
SAN JOSE, CALIFORNIA

Copyright

DEDICATION

To:

3 people - who I no longer see on earth but can't wait to spend eternity with: my dad, my mom, my beloved husband.

2 people - who inspire and motivate me to be the best I can be, Jeffery and Joshua. Mommy loves you.

1 person - who has been a constant through every season of my life. I love you big brother Troy!

0 - nly wise God who has brought me from breakdown to breakthrough!

CONTENTS

INTRODUCTION

*You're either in a storm, just coming out
of a storm, or heading into a storm.*

- Jeffery S. Heard

My late husband, Jeffery S. Heard, was a wise man. He often told me that storms, trials, and adversity affect everyone at some point in their lives. "In fact," he would say, "To live a life of no pain, suffering, or hardship is to not live at all."

You may have picked up this book because you're facing a storm or some insurmountable trial and feel as though you're on the verge of breaking down. Maybe someone gave you this book to help you through this difficult time. Maybe you're not in a trial right now, but you want to be better prepared for the next time you go through an adversity so that you'll finally experience a breakthrough instead of the usual breakdown. Whatever the reason you chose to read this book, my prayer is that you will find in it the keys to obtaining victory over adversity.

These keys aren't meant to simply provide useful infor-mation. They are powerful, practical, and proven steps that have helped me to persevere and overcome adversity in my life—adversity that exists even as I write this.

Only two months have passed since I knelt beside my five-year old son's seemingly lifeless body. He had fallen twenty feet out of a two-story window. I can still hear his agonizing moans as I tried to get him to respond to me. "Joshua, what happened?" I asked. He didn't answer. "Where are you hurt? Can you touch it?" He still didn't answer. The word "nightmare" comes to mind, but that word cannot describe what I experienced at his side or during the twenty-minute ambulance ride or while discussing his prognosis with the doctor.

My son suffered a fractured skull in two places, a severely broken wrist, and a bruised lung. He could have been paralyzed or sustained brain damage. The list of "could haves" is extremely long. But the bottom line is that God did an amazing miracle. He brought us through this adversity just as he has brought us through every other one. By the grace of God, Joshua has recovered.

The physical trauma for Joshua has mostly healed; but like most adversities, the aftermath has morphed into emotional damage—fear, worry, anxiety, and stress, especially for me. It's no wonder that spiritual and psychological counseling is so important in so many lives during painful times.

You may also be suffering from the aftermath of a terrible trauma, but this book is not specifically written to help you deal with these post-traumatic effects—although that is a secondary benefit. It's written to provide you with the keys to obtaining victory *during* your adversity, which will minimize the stress that often follows. In this way, the book is designed to serve as your coach during the middle of a challenging game to ensure that you will overcome the opposition and experience victory.

My prayer is that you will learn the keys to securing this victory and that God will strengthen and encourage you as you face the trials of your life so that you will move from breakdown to breakthrough.

CHAPTER 1

FIGHT OR FLIGHT

If you're going through hell, keep going.

~ Winston Churchill

I slammed the door, ran in the house, and hid behind the couch. At eight years old, I had never been more terrified than at that moment. I couldn't believe this was happening to me. Why would anyone want to hurt me? What did I do to deserve this? How will I ever make it out of the house alive again? These thoughts and many more ran through my mind as my mother peeked over the couch: "What's wrong? What happened?" She asked. All I could do was point out of the window. I couldn't bear the thought of repeating what happened to me.

I was in breakdown mode, a position I had been in so many other times in my life. I was hiding behind furniture at three years old when I saw my father stab my mother. I was here when I watched my brother beat my father out of

5

shear anger for abusing her. Yes, I was quite familiar with this position. I believed hiding was the only way to protect myself.

So what caused me to run and hide this time? Our family had just moved into the neighborhood. Many of the kids on the street asked if we could come outside and play, so my brother and I went into our backyard for a friendly game of kickball. While playing, several of the kids made fun of me. They pushed me "accidentally," and tried to trip me. Then the largest girl in the neighborhood said I hit her on purpose. When I say large, I'm speaking Goliath size, at least eight feet tall (so it seemed in my mind). She had to be at least twenty years old (Okay, a slight exaggeration), but she was certainly a teenager.

Before I could understand what was really happening, five kids tried to beat me up at once. They kicked me, scratched my face, and pulled my hair. I had never been in a fight before. I didn't know what to do. My older brother began to fight for me and as soon as I could, I did what any self-respecting kid in a neighborhood fight would do--I ran into the house and hid.

My mother followed my pointing finger out the window and screamed, "Oh, No!" She ran outside and stopped the fight. As I peeped outside, I thought to myself, "Whew at least that's over. Now I won't get hurt and neither will my brother." But my mother had another plan. She told all of the kids in the yard: "Okay, if you're going to fight my son, you can't fight him all at once. But you can let him beat you one at a time." So my mother allowed my brother to fight the neighborhood bullies one at a time.

The interesting thing is that he only had to fight one. The first one happened to be the biggest and the strongest.

When my brother beat him up, he didn't have to fight anyone else that day. Why in the world would a mother let her son stand there and fight? Clearly, this is not the *Focus on the Family,* Dr. James Dobson view of child rearing we hear about today. But my mother knew that if my brother didn't fight that day, he would have to fight on another day. She knew that he was safer fighting a fair fight with her present than an unfair fight with no help.

My brother and I faced a difficult decision that day. We had to choose whether we would face the adversity at hand and fight, or run away from it and take flight. I chose the latter. My brother chose the former. You have the same choice when you face trials and adversities in your life. You can fight or take flight. As we face adversities in our life, I believe that God encourages us to face our fears and fight through difficult circumstances. The blessing is that God promises to not only be there with us but also to fight our battles for us.

After that incident, I was afraid of fighting for a long time. But in sixth grade, I got a chance to fight the biggest bully in school. She was an eighth grader and ten feet tall (at least in my mind). This time, my brother wasn't around. I had nowhere to run, I had to face this challenge on my own. I tried everything I could to avoid the fight. This is what many of us do when we face adversity. We try to run away as soon as possible.

Sometimes, God will make you fight a fight you wish you could run away from. So I took my mother's advice: "In a fight, don't wait to be hit. Throw the first punch." By the grace of God, when I swung, I accidentally hit her. She tripped and fell to the ground. It looked like Goliath falling down; one swing and she rolled down the hill. Luckily, I landed on top of her and that was the end of that. From that moment on, I was no longer afraid to fight. Fighting gave me confidence to know that I didn't have to depend on anyone else to fight for me anymore, I could fight for myself.

In order to move from breakdown to breakthrough, we have to make a decision to face the adversity that exists in our life. Many times, we want to run because we don't want to deal with the pain. We don't want to be hurt emotionally, physically, or mentally anymore. We want to run and hide behind the couch and get in our "safe zone." But if we're going to experience breakthrough, we have to deal with the pain and face the fight head on.

No one enjoys being in pain. In fact, the worst physical pain I've ever experienced was giving birth. I can recall it as if it's happening now. Amidst the screams, I hear someone say, "You can do it. Don't give up. You can't quit. Just keep pushing. Don't stop now." At the most painful point of labor, when I wanted to give up the most, I felt I had no other choice but to keep pushing. When I decided to not run from but fight through the pain, God blessed me with the gift of a beautiful and amazing child.

Somehow, nature provides mothers with enough strength and energy to handle the pain and stress of childbirth. It's no different with trials and adversity. Like labor pains, we don't feel we can make it through, but somehow God provides each one of us with enough strength and energy to handle the spiritual, mental, physical, and emotional pain. If we don't give up but continue to push through the adversity, we will receive the blessings and the promises that God has planned for each of us. The challenge is knowing how to handle the pain during adversity. It's the pain that we run from. It's just a fact that if trials weren't painful, we would have no problem handling them.

Throughout this book, I'll provide several keys (like epidurals) to help you manage the adversity and its concurrent pain. I'll also provide encouragement (like a midwife) to help you keep on pushing through the pain until you receive your breakthrough and deliver victory in your life.

WHAT IS ADVERSITY?

Before learning how to deal with adversity, let's first understand what it is. For the purpose of this book, adversity is something that comes against you, your purpose, your direction, the reason God created you. Jeremiah 29:11 says, "'For I know the plans I have for you,' declares the Lord, 'plans to prosper you and not to harm you, plans to give you hope and a future.'" Contrary to God's promise, adversity comes into your life to resist God's plans and purposes for you. It opposes your goals, vision, or destiny and, instead, brings about an unfavorable or antagonistic effect in your life.

The word "adversity" comes from the word "adverse" where we also get the word "versus." Adversity then, is like the struggle between two football teams playing against each other at the Rose Bowl or two soccer teams competing for the World Cup. Each side has the goal of victory and works toward advancing it with a focused strength. In a similar way, you are in a constant struggle reaching for the prize in spite of opposing forces.

FORMS OF ADVERSITY

Adversity reveals itself in three ways: (1) common calamities or natural disasters from outside forces, such as hurricanes, tornadoes, and earthquakes, (2) inner desires that cause us to make unwise relationship choices, health choices, or career moves, and` (3) demonic forces such as injury, accidents, loss of job, diseases, negative people, or unhealthy relationships. This third form is an opposing force that generally originates with Satan who tries to accuse or destroy the testimony of a believer. He uses these trials to cause you to doubt the promises of God and to get you to walk away from God's divine purpose in your life.

Like an opposing team, Satan is your adversary with two primary goals. First, he wants to keep you away from developing a relationship with Jesus Christ so that you won't enter heaven. But the incredible news is that Jesus destroyed the work of the enemy on the cross and forever prevented Satan from defeating those who accept Jesus as Lord and Savior. He can't take away your eternal inheritance if you truly believe in Jesus.

If you have never asked Jesus to be your Savior, then now is your chance to claim victory over Satan in this area of your life. Jesus Christ died on the cross, was buried, and rose again on the third day so that you may receive forgiveness of your sin and enter eternal life. There is no sin too great or small that God will not forgive.

Romans 10:9 says that "if you confess with your mouth, 'Jesus is Lord,' and believe in your heart that God raised him from the dead, you will be saved.'" If you would like to confess that Jesus is your Lord and ask him to save you from the traps of the enemy, then pray this simple prayer.

> Lord Jesus, I am a sinner in need of a Savior. Forgive me of my sins. I believe that you died on the cross, was buried, and rose again on the third day for the forgiveness of sin. Now, Jesus, enter my heart and help me to live for you. In Jesus' name, Amen.

If you prayed this prayer for the first time, let me be the first to congratulate you and say, "Welcome to the kingdom of God." Because you believe that Jesus forgave your sins through his blood, you have just had your very first victory over Satan. I encourage you to contact a Christian friend and let him or her know about your decision. You can also contact me at the number and/or website address listed on the back of this book.

Be assured that once you have given your life to Jesus Christ, the enemy can no longer keep you from going to heaven. Your salvation is sealed in the blood of Jesus. However, Satan does have a second goal, which he can succeed at if we let him. He tries to destroy the amazing life that God desires each of us to have. Christ warned that "the thief comes only to steal and kill and destroy; I have come that they may have life, and have it to the full" (John 10:10). Satan is this thief who tries to steal, kill, and destroy the abundant life that Jesus Christ has promised each of us. How does he do this? Each time we face adversity, Satan uses it to discourage us, make us feel helpless and defeated. He makes it seem as though walking with God is not working for us. Through that discouragement, he also tries to destroy our testimony to others.

I wish someone had warned me about this adversity when I first gave my life to Jesus Christ. Instead, I was given the impression that being saved meant I would be free from troubles and walk on rose pedals all the way to heaven. Nobody said that it might even get harder. As a matter of fact, once we give our life to Jesus Christ we have just signed up to be attacked because we are no longer on Satan's team but on God's.

What are some of these attacks that Satan, our opponent will use? We might experience depression, marital problems, disease, divorce, sickness, financial calamity, death in the family, health problems, friends leaving you, or difficulty in the work place, just to name a few.

Adversity is no respecter of persons either. The apostle Peter wrote this to new Christians: "Dear friends, do not be surprised at the painful trial you are suffering, as though something strange were happening to you" (1 Peter 4:12). Everyone, whether they are saved or not, will face adversity. It's not some strange occurrence; but rather, we need to see it as a normal part of living life. However, just because we experience adversity, that does not mean adversity has to destroy us. Having a relationship with Jesus Christ provides us the hope and tools we need to experience victory in our adversity.

Purpose of Adversity

God uses adversity to make us better; Satan uses adversity to make us bitter. This bitterness encourages us to quit our God-given plans and destiny. However, there's so much good that God can and will do as a result of our trials. The apostle Paul says, "We know that in all things God works for the good of those who love him" (Romans 8:28). "All things" means the good things and the bad things. In other words, God is working this trial and adversity for our good: we will draw closer to God, making us stronger, wiser, and more prepared for our future

The real issue with adversity is not whether we will have it, but what will we do when we face it. There are really only two responses: we can either run away and avoid it, or we can deal with it head on. It's the fight or flight syndrome again.

Unfortunately, I've never heard anyone say, "I'm so excited to be going through hell right now. It's so much fun." No. If we're truly honest, each of us probably says something like this during our trials: "Forget it. I give up. I don't want to deal with the pressure. It's too hard." Or we might say,

"Why me? Why do I have to be the one facing this issue?" Another response might be: "Why now? This adversity is interrupting my plans and my purpose." Remember, if Satan is involved, adversity will oppose your purpose, plans, or directions because that's his purpose, too.

This opposition looks something like this: I'm minding my own business. I have my purpose, my destiny, my dreams, my visions, my hopes, my family, my job, my future all planned out. I am focused and nothing is going to stop me (see Figure 1A).

Then I run into adversity. I lose my job. My spouse wants a divorce. I find out I have cancer. A family member dies. Adversity is anything that presents a roadblock to the destiny and purpose that God has for me (see Figure 1B).

I'm now at a crossroads. If I decide to run, then what I'm really doing is getting off course from the destiny and direction God has for me. I may either never get back on track or it may take me a lot longer with a lot more headaches to reach God's purpose in my life (see Figure 1C).

However, if I choose to fight and face the adversity head on, I will reach the destination a lot faster. I will come out stronger because I continued to fight (see Figure 1D).

When adversity hits like this, don't say, "I'm walking away. I quit. I give up." If you falter, you have no strength and fail to build any new strength to handle future issues. If you keep pressing on, you gain strength like a bodybuilder who gets stronger by exercising his muscles. It hurts during the process; but ultimately, you become stronger because of the process.

We often quit from loss of hope and faith that our situations can get better. We give up when we decide that God isn't working to change our lives for the better. We falter and stop progressing toward our goal when we break down and

DEALING WITH ADVERSITY—A VISUAL OVERVIEW

FIGURE 1A: BEFORE ADVERSITY

FIGURE 1B: ADVERSITY STRIKES

FIGURE 1C: OPTION 1 - FLIGHT FROM ADVERSITY

FIGURE 1D: OPTION 2 – FIGHT ADVERSITY

decide that, like a car stalled on the side of the road, there's nothing more we can do so we might as well surrender our lives to the circumstance. Instead, we need to take charge of our lives and our destiny by trusting in God, by continuing to fight for our breakthrough and for the promises of God in our lives.

In this regard, keep in mind Proverbs 24:10 that says, "If you falter in times of trouble, how small is your strength!" The word "falter" actually means to lose strength or momentum, to relax or become slack. If you walk away from the adversities in your life, you lose momentum toward your goals, visions, and destiny.

At the start of a race, the last thing the runners are told is, "Don't stop," because if they stop, it's very hard to start running again. They lose momentum. When we take a break from praying, attending church, reading the word, seeking God, being around positive influences, or hoping in God for a change, we lose momentum in the race to receive God's promises for us. Once we go off course and stop our momentum, it's much harder to start all over again. But if we continue to do the things God called us to do, even when we hit adversity, we will not falter and lose our strength. As the old saying goes, "It's easier to move a rolling rock than a stagnant one."

Blessings often come from adversity, so I encourage you not to lose your momentum. Don't relax. Don't give up. Whatever trials you are facing, hang in there, God has a promise and a blessing on the other side. Don't let life cause you to break down on the side of the road and quit. You will never experience your breakthrough and give birth to your destiny, your purpose, your visions if you quit.

Sometimes, instead of running away from it or through it, we try to figure a way around our adversity. Our minds begin to think of possible solutions. We research the internet, talk to friends, or seek professional counselors who tell us how to solve our problems. In many cases, their solutions can result in further headaches and difficulties. Does this mean that we're supposed to do nothing? Of course not. There are some specific steps we can take to gain victory over our adversity. Paul tells us what these are in Ephesians 6:10-18:

> Finally, be strong in the Lord and in his mighty power. Put on the full armor of God so that you can take your stand against the devil's schemes. For our struggle is not against flesh and blood, but against the rulers, against the authorities, against the powers of this dark world and against the spiritual forces of evil in the heavenly realms.
>
> Therefore put on the full armor of God, so that when the day of evil comes, you may be able to stand your ground, and after you have done everything, to stand. *Stand firm* then, with *the belt of truth* buckled around your waist, with *the breastplate of righteousness* in place, and with your feet fitted with the readiness that comes from the *gospel of peace*. In addition to all this, take up the *shield of faith*, with which you can extinguish all the flaming arrows of the evil one. Take the *helmet of salvation* and the sword of the Spirit, which is the word of God. And *pray in the Spirit* on all occasions with all kinds of prayers and requests (italics added).

The best way for us to fight through adversity is to put on the full armor. Chapters 4 to 10 explain how to use each piece of armor as keys to victory over the battle. This battle wages with external and internal enemies. So, before giving you the keys to battling the outside enemy, let's look at how to overcome our inner enemy.

CHAPTER 2

FIGHTING THE ENEMY IN ME

Much of your pain is self-chosen.

- Kahlil Gibran

As a single, college student in my late teens, I tried to live obediently to God and remain celibate. While teaching Bible study to my peers, the Lord convicted me that having sex before marriage was wrong and not honoring to him. So I decided that I would not have sex again until I got married. I vowed to God, "I'm not going to give up my cookies until the man buys the cow that produces the milk to go with the cookies." With that said, I was all set to live my vow of celibacy before the Lord.

There was only one problem, I had a boyfriend at the time and I actually liked giving my cookies away. That put me in a conundrum. I felt just like Paul who said, "I have the desire to do what is good, but I cannot carry it out. For what I do is not the good I want to do; no, the evil I do not want to do—this I keep on doing" (Romans 7:18-19).

No matter how many times I vowed not to sin, somehow, I kept on doing it and asking God to forgive me. I felt so horrible about myself. I hated that I said one thing to my peers and lived another. It seemed like the vow-breaking and the tremendous, internal conflict would never end. Then a breakthrough came. I would obey God for days at a time, maybe even a month. I'd pat myself on the back and think, "Hallelujah, I've finally overcome. I'm never going back to that old lifestyle." Then, before I knew it, I was back on my knees weeping before God because I had fallen yet again.

How do we gain victory over the internal adversity that sin creates within us? How do we move beyond the point where we overcome for a few days, weeks, or even months and then fall back into the same pattern of sin again? I got so tired of committing to God that I would never have sex again, and then falling on my face repenting because I just had sex again. I wanted a way out.

Now before I tell you the way out, I want to assure you that there is hope in your situation. No matter what you are dealing with, you can overcome the enemy within you and have victory over sin. How do I know? Before I got married, I remained celibate for five years. Now, I am a widow and since the day my husband passed away, I have remained celibate. We can have victory over our sin—*even those sins that we commit over and over again.*

How do we break the cycle of sin and gain victory? While writing this book I have been hoping and praying that the Lord would give me a three-step solution to solving all of our sin problems. After all, I enjoy watching *The Biggest Loser* and *Extreme Makeover* shows because they offer quick solutions to obesity and home decay. I prayed that God would provide a simple approach to ridding sin in our lives as well. But God didn't do that. Sometimes he doesn't work that way.

Unfortunately, victory over sin is not found in a one-hour episode or a seven-day vacation. If you know of a quick or simple solution, please write, email, or call me as soon as possible. As far as I know, there are no pills to take, no magic wands to wave, no person to lay hands on us in order to instantly alleviate the sin that we have wrestled with for years.

To try to speed up the victory, we often try to solve the symptoms of sin without dealing with its root cause. For instance, when we have a cough, we buy cough drops. We think we are treating the root cause, but really we are only alleviating the symptom. We could be coughing for several reasons: maybe we have allergies or a head cold or lung cancer or digestive problems. We don't know what the root cause is, but we take over-the-counter cough medicine anyway. The cough goes away for a few days, but often comes back even stronger.

So it is with sin. When we don't know the root cause, we continue to sin. We might find a way to stop for a little while, thinking we have gained victory; but in reality, we just masked a solution for the moment and never truly experienced a full healing or complete victory.

For many of us, we know exactly what to do to overcome our nagging sin. We know that to lose weight, we need to stop eating fatty foods. We know we need to leave that person who is hurting us. We know we need to stop lying, cheating, stealing, using drugs/alcohol, or treating people nasty.

However, we struggle to translate that head knowledge into actual victory over sin. It can take several years for us to get out of our old sin habits. There are some people who God can heal miraculously, however, if we have been struggling and praying and asking God for help and nothing has changed permanently, then we have to stop waiting on the magic pill or surgery or someone to lay hands on us. We have to take some action to change the things in our lives that is causing the adversity. In order to conquer sin, we must actively pursue a change in our lifestyle. We have to change our choices, habits, and attitudes toward the sin in our lives. We have to work at making changes and having victory over our sin—and that work starts with understanding what Jesus did for us.

The apostle John explained this work well when he said, "You know that he appeared so that he might take away our sins" (John 3:5). Jesus Christ came not only to cancel the *penalty* of sin in our life but he also came to cancel the *power* of sin in our life. Regarding the penalty, we're all sinners and deserve death as punishment for our sins (Romans 3:23, 6:23). Death is being eternally separated from God and entering hell. Our sin deserves the punishment of hell. However, Jesus Christ died on the cross to pay the penalty we were supposed to pay. Jesus shed his blood so that we no longer have to suffer condemnation for our sins or fear a future in hell, separated from him forever.

Because we have disobeyed God's laws, we deserve death, but God is a loving and forgiving God. He has great compassion and mercy on each of us. Lamentations 3:22-23 says, "It is of the Lord's mercies that we are not consumed because his compassions fail not. They are new every morning: great is thy faithfulness." I'm so glad that the Lord has new mercy, compassion, and faithfulness for me each day (no matter how often I sin).

No matter what we have done in the past, no matter how awful it may seem, no matter how much pain we have caused, Jesus Christ forgave us of our sin. The amazing promise of Jesus Christ is that "if we confess our sins, he is faithful and just and will forgive us our sins and purify us from all unrighteousness" (1 John 1:9). Not only does Jesus forgive us but he removes our sins as far as the east is from the west (Psalms 103:12). God takes our sins, throws them into the sea of forgetfulness and remembers them no more (Hebrews 10:17).

Our confession removes the penalty of death attached to our sin, but it does not remove the consequences of sin or the desire to repeat it. Yes, Jesus forgave me for having sex outside of marriage, but my confession didn't remove the desire to want to have sex again or the consequence of getting pregnant.

We often beat ourselves up over sins that God doesn't remember. It's time for us to stop allowing Satan to emotionally and verbally abuse us. He's an accuser who spends his time reminding us of our sin. He tells us we are no good, horrible, unworthy, and worthless. One of his famous accusations is, "You'll never change." That is such a lie! Once we've made Jesus Christ Lord of our lives, we become a new creation in Christ Jesus. The old self goes away and the new self comes (2 Cor. 5:17).

Don't believe what the enemy says. God will convict us of our sin, but he will not condemn us for it. In other words we might feel guilty about *what we've done*, but Satan makes us feel guilty about *who we are*. Always keep in mind that "there is now no condemnation for those who are in Christ

Jesus" (Romans 8:1). Anytime you begin to feel bad about *who* you are, remind yourself *whose* you are.

Whenever I get down on myself or whenever the enemy brings accusations against me, I recite an affirmation. Affirmations may be true of who you are now or of who you desire to become. Our minds and body will often follow that which we speak about ourselves, so if spoken constantly, affirmations have the power to transform our words into reality. Here are my affirmations, but they apply to every believer as well:

· I am chosen by God (Colossians 3:12).

• I am a new creation in Christ Jesus (2 Corinthians 5:17)

• I am the righteousness of God (2 Corinthians 5:21)

• I am a royal priesthood, a holy nation, a person belonging to God (2 Peter 2:9)

• I am fearfully and wonderfully made (Psalms 139:14)

• I am deeply loved, totally accepted and completely forgiven by God (Ephesians 1:7-8)

Never let the enemy cause you to think less of yourself. Instead, see yourself the way God sees you. Remember that condemnation is not from God—it's from Satan.

Now that we understand we have victory over sin in Jesus Christ and that the penalty of sin (death) was paid for by Jesus on the cross, we're left with a resounding question: why do we still sin? The apostle John says that "no one who is born of God will continue to sin, because God's seed remains in him; he cannot go on sinning" (1 John 3:9). That seems to be a contradiction in the life of the believer. If we are truly saved, we wouldn't continue to sin. However, we know we are saved and, yet, we still sin. Does the fact that we continue to sin mean that we are not born of God—that we are not truly saved?

While having sex outside of marriage, I wondered, too, if I was saved and forgiven. This doubt stirred up a major, internal adversity for me. Many of you reading this book may be feeling the same way. You are saved. You know you are forgiven. Yet, you constantly struggle with committing the same sin over and over again. You may have even prayed, "Oh, Lord, forgive me for committing this sin. I promise I will never do it again." A few days later you say it again. As a matter of fact, if you are like me, you have asked for forgiveness over the same sin so often that you might as well record your confession and hit the play button several times a day.

Instead of feeling victorious over the sin, it feels more like we're chained in bondage to it. How frustrating. We want to quit. We try to quit. But we can't. Maybe the sin is anger, pornography, lust, poor relationships, bitterness, selfishness, pride, greed, overspending, overeating, or thousands of other vices. Like a drug or alcohol addiction, something keeps pulling us back into it. Sin, the flesh and our own desires, wants to master us.

When we can't let the sin go, it succeeds in its mastery. But as believers, we must be assured that the final victory is won because of the blood of Jesus. He saves us from the eternal bondage in hell that sin requires. However, Satan does not want us to receive that sane victory on earth. He tries to get sin to master us now so that we don't experience the abundant life that Jesus wants to give believers.

THE KEY TO VICTORY OVER SIN - REPENTANCE

The key to obtaining victory over our sin is found in one word, *repentance*. If we really and truly repent, we will not continue to live a lifestyle of sin because repentance means a change of mind. It is a decision to turn away from our lifestyle of sin. Repentance is a choice to obey God's desires and not our own. It is a determination that no matter what, we will not commit that act of disobedience to God again. It is a deliberate exercise of our will in which we determine that we are going to act differently in the future than we have in the past.

Repentance is completely different from confession. The reason we continue to struggle with sin and don't have victory over it is that we have confessed often but we have not repented. Confession means that we agree with God that we are wrong and ask God to forgive us. We can confess but never really turn away from our sins. *Believers are great at confession and horrible at repentance.*

For instance, we can pray every night before we go to bed: "Lord, forgive me of my sins. The sins that I know about and the ones I don't know about." Then tomorrow, we commit the same sins all over again. Why? Because we only confessed; we didn't truly repent. We didn't make a decision to actually turn away from those sins, never to go back and commit them again.

Once I truly repented, turned away from having sex outside of marriage, and made the choice never to go back, only then was I set free. When I became a widow, the issue of sex outside of marriage was null and void for me because true repentance means never going back. It doesn't mean we won't be tempted. It means we make a final decision to set our will to never return to our old ways.

Turning away from sin for good is not easy; but by using these six keys, true repentance can become a reality:

KEY 1: HEAR THE VOICE OF CORRECTION

God will always communicate with us when we are in the midst of committing a sin. He will use pastors, teachers, spiritual leaders, the Bible, friends, family, television, radio, nature, or anything necessary to convict us and correct us of our disobedience. He does this because he doesn't want us to be oblivious to our sin; he desires that we recognize it and turn away from it. Second Kings 17:13 says,

> The Lord warned Israel and Judah through all his prophets and seers:"Turn from your evil ways. Observe my commands and decrees, in accordance with the entire Law that I commanded your fathers to obey and that I delivered to you through my servants the prophets."

When we hear the voice of correction, we have arrived at a decision point. We must decide whether or not we will heed the direction to obey God or continue to sin. Many people call this voice our conscience. They say our conscience directs us to do right or wrong. However, as believers, the still, small voice telling us what pleases God and what doesn't is the Holy Spirit living inside us, not our conscience.

KEY 2: ALLOW YOURSELF TO BE CORRECTED

A truly repentant heart will not walk away from the voice of God; it will walk away from sin. Therefore, we must allow the words of God to penetrate our heart and correct our sinful way. Second Timothy 3:16-17 says, "All Scripture is

God-breathed and is useful for teaching, rebuking, correcting and training in righteousness, so that the man of God may be thoroughly equipped for every good work."

Therefore, if we truly want to have victory over sin, we have to listen to the hard teaching, rebuking, and correcting about our sin. Many people don't like preachers and teachers who talk like that. They prefer to focus on trying to get a blessing, achieving prosperity, and living the abundant life. But if we really want to have victory, we must stop running away from those who are speaking the truth about our sin.

Don't turn off a preacher who teaches about topics that are difficult to hear, such as gossip, pride, overindulgence, and lust; instead, open your ears even wider and hear the word of God coming in. God doesn't send these difficult messages to hurt or condemn us. He sends them to correct our behavior. He's saying that it's time to deal with that issue of sin in our life.

Don't get discouraged, either, if every time you open your Bible you feel condemned about a particular sin. That is God saying he is getting ready to help you have victory over that particular issue.

In addition to hearing God's Word on the matter, you may need an accountability partner to keep you on the path to victory. This is someone whom you can call when you feel tempted to sin, who won't judge you or make you feel bad about your struggle. This person can encourage you and pray for you to turn away from the sin once and for all. An accountability partner can be someone who is struggling in the same area or has already obtained their victory. Above, all, he or she must be strong in the word of God and able to provide you with spiritual strength.

KEY 3: RESPOND, DON'T RUN

Our natural inclination is to run away from difficult circumstances. However, running away from sin never really solves the problem. The real issue is this: how do we respond to sin in our life as we deal with it? The primary answer is that God invites us to talk to him about our sin issue. Isaiah 1:18 says,

> Come now, let us reason together, says the Lord. Though your sins are like scarlet, they shall be as white as snow; though they are red as crimson, they shall be like wool.

The best way to respond to sin without running from it is to talk to Jesus about it. The talk should seek answers to the following questions:

- Why do I like this sin so much?

- Why is it so very hard for me to stop?

- Do I still want to continue to do this sin?

- How do I truly feel after I've committed this sin?

We might not receive solid answers to any of these questions right away, but as we begin to talk with Jesus—as though we're talking to a friend about our problems—he begins to bring clarity to our sin situation. During this conversation, it's vital to be honest, open, and vulnerable. God already knows the truth to these answers even when we don't, so there is really no reason to lie.

When we tell Jesus the truth about our sin issue, self-discovery flourishes. Often we discover that we really like committing the sin. If that is the case, then no amount of confession will give us victory over it. We enjoy what we are doing so much that giving it up is like giving up our favorite toy or car or pet. It induces feelings of loss, sadness, or even depression because we think we gave up something quite valuable, yet gained nothing for God.

While struggling with my decision to remain celibate, for example, I had to get real with God. I told him, "I enjoy sex. I like it and I will probably do it again." Yes, I said it. I told the Lord that I enjoyed it so much that, given another opportunity, I would say yes to sin and no to him. I know that doesn't sound very Christian, but it's the truth and that's what God is looking for. He's not looking for religious answers; he wants the truth of what's in our hearts. Reasoning with God means telling him *everything* in your heart without restraint.

KEY 4: AGREE WITH GOD

Just because we're truthful with God about our sin, doesn't mean that God will change his viewpoint about it. He's waiting for us to admit to him that what we're doing is wrong. As a wise man said, "He who conceals his sins does not prosper, but whoever *confesses and renounces* them finds mercy" (Proverbs 28:13, italics added).

Confession means to agree with God, to say to him, "Lord, I agree that I have sinned and I am wrong." Instead, of justifying our actions, let us acknowledge our sin before the living God because "if we claim to be without sin, we deceive ourselves and the truth is not in us. If we confess our sins, he is faithful and just and will forgive us our sins and purify us from all unrighteousness" (1 John 1:8-9).

KEY 5: EXPRESS GENUINE SORROW

We should be genuinely upset and sorrowful over the sin we have committed. In fact, if we have not arrived at the point where we feel utterly sick and tired of our sin, we're not ready to repent. In other words, if we continue to delight in our sin, then we'll find it difficult to quit. We'll feel as if God is depriving us of something good.

In my case, every time I had sex, I felt dirty, yucky, and filthy. The momentary pleasure wasn't worth the days and weeks of disgust I felt for disobeying God. Until we dislike the sin—even have a downright revulsion and hatred for it—we won't be able to truly repent and have victory.

How do we learn to hate something we love? We can only do it with God's help. I asked God to take away my desire for sex outside of marriage. I asked him to make the act seem so deplorable that my stomach would turn with nauseous convulsions at the thought of it. I asked God to do this for me so that I could honor him. And he did. He reversed my joy and pain sensors. It was almost a spiritual "Pavlov's dog" experience.

Pavlov was a psychologist who experimented with conditional reflexes in dogs and humans. He concluded that we are conditioned to respond in similar ways each time we are presented with a stimuli. God desires for us to be conditioned to respond in obedience to the stimulus of his word and get upset when we are faced with the option of disobeying him—committing sin. "'Even now,' declares the Lord, 'return to me with all your heart, with fasting and weeping and mourning'" (Joel 2:12). God desires us to return to him with genuine mourning and weeping over our sin issue.

Paul wrote to Christians mourning over their sins: "See what this godly sorrow has produced in you: what earnestness, what eagerness to clear yourselves, what indignation, what alarm, what longing, what concern, what readiness to see justice done" (2 Corinthians 7:11). With godly sorrow, we will *want to* do whatever it takes to deal with the situation, be healed, and clear ourselves of this sin.

KEY 6: TURN AWAY FROM SIN

The final key to obtaining victory over sin is to turn away from it and keep on turning away from it. Isaiah 1:16-17 says, "Stop doing wrong, learn to do right!" I know that sounds ridiculously easy and especially hard at the same time—and it is.

When I was struggling with my commitment to remain celibate, I met my "ideal partner." He looked right, talked right, and dressed right. We exchanged phone numbers, and I knew that if I ever saw this man again, I would not fulfill my desire to be obedient to God. I remember coming home the night I received his phone number. I got on my knees and prayed, "Lord, don't let me ever see this man again. If I see him I am going to have sex with him. He's my type and I am weak for that type. God don't let him call me."

That night I reasoned with God about my potential to sin. God gave me the strength to rip up his number into tiny pieces, just in case I got weak before the trash man came. I never heard from or saw this man again. I am so grateful that the Lord answered my prayer.

We can't depend on our own strength to keep us from falling. So before the fall, we must ask God to give us a way out. He will always give us the strength to walk away from sin, as long as we seek him and look for it.

When we finally stop doing wrong; we must learn to do what is right. We must replace the sin with a positive activity or thought that draws us closer to God. If not, we will likely fall right back into the same adversity and turmoil.

Jesus helps us know what we ought to be thinking about when he says, "I am the vine; you are the branches. *If a man remains in me and I in him, he will bear much fruit; apart from me you can do nothing"* (John 15:5, italics added). *Remaining in Christ* is the abiding principle. It means to spend time in his word, meditate on his word, pray to him, worship him, and fellowship with other believers. We will take a look at how to abide in the word of God and remain in Christ in chapter 10.

If you use these keys, you can experience a personal breakthrough over sin and have victory over internal adversity in your life.

CHAPTER 3

TOO SCARED
TO STAND FIRM
(Stand Firm in the Faith)

*Do not be afraid. Stand firm and you will see
the deliverance the Lord will bring you today.
The Egyptians you see today you will never see again.*

~ Exodus 14:13

On Christmas Day of 2008, four young men taunted and teased a 350-pound tiger at the San Francisco Zoo. The tiger escaped its confines and charged after the men, killing one and mauling another. What would you do if a 350-pound tiger charged at you? Where would you get the strength to fight or stand firm against such an attacker?

Thankfully, few people will ever face that situation. However, every day, you and I face spiritual attacks from circumstances, situations, and problems that feel as if that 350-pound tiger is hunting us down. This is normal. In fact, the Bible says that our enemy, the devil, prowls around looking for someone to devour (1 Peter 5:8).

The word "devour" in Greek is *katapinō*. It means "to suffer ruin or destruction, overwhelm with grief, to cause the complete cessation or to drown."[1] Our adversary's purpose is to cause us to come into complete ruin and one way he does this is to overwhelm us with grief. Sometimes the adversity in our life is so difficult that we feel as if we're ready to die or at least walk away from the promises of God. That is Satan's plan—to annihilate us and destroy us if not on earth while alive then in hell after we're dead. However, God has a plan to help us deal with this type of attack.

God's plan is similar to the instructions that rangers give hikers in game parks where it's possible to confront lions and other wild animals. The guide will say, "What I am about to tell you is very important, so listen carefully: while on the hike, we might come across a lion."

At this point, they are a bit afraid but realize this is a part of hiking in a wild area.

The guide continues, "If you come across a lion, whatever you do, don't turn around and run. Do you understand?"

The people look at each other, then back at him: "Yeah."

"Even if he charges at you, *do not turn and run*. Just stand still. Look him straight in the eye and wait."

It's certainly not my first thought to stand still and watch a wild lion charge at me. But this is the best advice in the middle of a tremendous adversity. It's also the same advice Peter gave to the first Christians. First he told them that Satan is roaring around like a lion looking for someone to devour. Then he advised, "Resist him, standing firm in the faith, because you know that your brothers throughout the world are undergoing the same kind of sufferings" (1 Peter 5:9).

God's plan for us as we deal with the attack of the enemy is to stand firm. Of course, this isn't easy. How can you stand firm when faced with cancer, loss of a love one, loss of a job, or a bitter divorce?

What does it really mean to stand firm in these situations? It means that, during a trial, we won't move from our faith or position in Jesus Christ as a child of God, his heir, deeply loved, wonderfully made, and totally accepted. During adversity we must stand on the promises of God (his word), on the blood of Jesus Christ, and on the hope that rests on God. We can't be moved and overwhelmed with worry, frustration, fear, grief, or any other negative emotion. Our strength must be in the Lord. Paul tells us how to do that:

> Be strong in the Lord and in his mighty power. Put on the full armor of God so that you can take your stand against the devil's schemes for our struggle is not against flesh and blood, but against the rulers, against the authorities, against the powers of this dark world and against the spiritual forces of evil in the heavenly realms. Therefore put on the full armor of God, so that when the day of evil comes, you may be able to stand your ground, and after you have done everything, to stand. *Stand firm then, with the belt of truth* buckled around your waist, *with the breastplate of righteousness in place* (Ephesians 6:10-14, italics added).

This word "stand" means to maintain our ground, to not yield or flee. It means to make firm, fix, or establish; to hold our position against an adversary. It also means to persevere, to stand fast and to stand firm. Maintaining our position is vital to winning any battle. Our position is based upon what God has said to us during the battle. We can't stop praying, worshipping, reading the word, or seeking God during difficult times. When we stop doing these things, we forget to listen to God and don't hear his words—words that will encourage us during battle.

Standing firm is being in a position to hear God's voice and stand on his promises. We get out of position when we focus on our own ability to confront and overcome the enemy. But when our focus is on I, me, and my, we lose sight of Jesus' power and ability to give us victory.

We must stand on the promises of God (his word) and not our own because nothing else lasts forever: "The grass withers and the flowers fall, but the word of our God stands forever" (Isaiah 40:8). We must stand firm during the battle, holding God's sword (his word), and believe in its power and strength because "God is not a man, that he should lie, nor a son of man, that he should change his mind. Does he speak and then not act? Does he promise and not fulfill?" (Numbers 23:19). The answer is no. We can stand firm on God's word during battle because he always keeps his promises.

Don't worry if God has given you a promise, but you don't know how it's going to be fulfilled. Often God will give us a promise without telling us how he will accomplish it. He does this because we are designed to live on God's promises not on God's explanations. Jesus said so:

> Therefore everyone who hears these words of mine and puts them into practice is like a wise man who built his house on the rock. The rain came down, the streams rose, and the winds blew and beat against that house; yet it did not fall, because it had its foundation on the rock (Matthew 7:24-25).

Standing firm means to maintain our faith and trust in God, believing that his promises will come to pass in our life. Our faith is also in the rock of Jesus Christ. We don't stand firm in our own strength or ability but in the strength and ability of Jesus, our rock. To stand firm on the rock of Jesus means that we put our faith, hope, and trust in someone who is completely immovable, unshakable, and unchanging. Although the storms will come in our life, if we stand firm on Jesus Christ and on God's word, we will be able to stand against the test and the trials of our life.

Why does this work? Because the real key to standing firm is expressed in Ephesians 6:10: "Be strong in the Lord and in his mighty power." Don't try to fight the enemy or solve your problems in your own power. We often make problems worse when we try to fix them without going to God first. It's almost like trying to assemble a complicated piece of furniture without ever reading the instruction manual. After a lot of frustration, it may look like all the pieces fit together; but under pressure, it will fall apart.

To be strong, we have to be made strong because we don't have the strength to fight off the 350-pound tiger by ourselves. But thanks be to God, we can be made strong through one who is stronger than the tiger. Greater is our God who lives inside of us than the roaring lion that is trying to devour us. Our external source of strength is Jesus Christ. Jesus will supply all the strength that we need in the midst of our trials and circumstances. The psalmist reveals his source of strength in Psalm 27:1-3:

> The Lord is the stronghold of my life
>   – of whom shall I be afraid?
> When evil men advance against me
>   to devour my flesh,
> when my enemies and my foes attack me,
>   they will stumble and fall.
> Though an army besiege me,
>   My heart will not fear;
> though war break out against me,
>   even then will I be confident.

Apart from Jesus, our efforts are futile. We can't heal, restore, deliver, or fix anything in our own strength. Even if we think we can, our knowledge, creativity, and resources all come from God. That's why Philippians 4:13 is so powerful to remember during times of adversity: "I can do all things through Christ who strengthens me." Paul wrote that while in prison for his faith. Paul also wrote to fellow Christians, praying that they would know God's incomparably great power:

> That power is like the working of his mighty strength, which he exerted in Christ when he raised him from the dead and seated him at his right hand in the heavenly realms, far above all rule and authority, power and dominion, and every title that can be given, not only in the present age but also in the one to come (Ephesians 1:19-21).

The Lord's power and might are infinite. By his strength, God not only created the heavens and the earth, caused the mountains to tremble, the rocks to melt, Jordan to be driven back, the cedars of Lebanon to be broken in pieces, and the forests to be stripped bare; but by his strength, he caused Jesus Christ to rise from the dead. This same power that caused Jesus to rise from the dead is available to you and me.

God is able to take situations that seem as though they're dead and turn them around. He is able to bring healing after the doctor says nothing more can be done. He is able to provide a job in a recession. He is able to heal a marriage that is heading for divorce. He is able to save a child that is on drugs or in jail. God is able and has the power to change every situation. Stop looking at what you can do and start looking at what God can do.

Once you realize that victory comes with God's power and might and not our own, then we only need to stand firm and be still, just as Exodus 14:13-14 says, "Do not be afraid. Stand firm and you will see the deliverance the Lord will bring you today. The Egyptians you see today you will never see again. The Lord will fight for you; you need only to be still." That's why Paul says in Ephesians 6:13 that we are to stand firm as we equip ourselves for battle with God's armor.

To stand firm on Jesus is to partner with him in the battle. Several years ago, an NBA rookie, Stacey King, played with Michael Jordan. During one phenomenal game, Jordan scored a resounding sixty-nine points. The rookie stayed on the bench until the last minutes of the game. During the last few seconds, the rookie made one free throw and scored a whopping one point. In a post-game interview, the rookie, Stacey King seemed to be extremely pleased with his performance. He is quoted as saying, "Together Michael Jordan and I scored seventy points."

This is how our relationship with Jesus Christ works. Dr. James Dobson says, "We are just rookies playing with the Legend. As long as he blesses our meager talent, it will be sufficient."[2] With God, we become the majority. With God, we can change the world. With God, we can weather any storm. As long as we stand firm in the Lord, he will take our inadequacies and infuse us with His strength so that we accomplish his will and his purpose in our life.

Remember, at some time in your life, you'll hear the lion roar; and when he charges toward you, stand firm and keep on standing. As we continue on our journey to victory, we will look at each piece of the armor of God as a vital component to not only standing firm, but obtaining our victory in Jesus Christ. Let's begin assembling our armament.

CHAPTER 4

LORD, I DON'T WANT TO TALK TO YOU
(PRAY)

*Evening and morning and at noon
I will pray and cry aloud
and He shall hear my voice*

~ Psalms 55:17, NKJV

Seven days after my first child was born, my mother died. She would have been his only living grandparent. My husband's parents died before he was nineteen and my father had been dead for three years. While I was seven months pregnant my mother was diagnosed with stage four stomach cancer. At the time, I was a pastor's wife. I believed God. I prayed for her healing. I knew God was able to heal. Yet somehow, she still died.

The anger, pain, and stress felt unbearable. "Not my mother, God. You can have anyone else but not her." I cried. "As a new mother, I need my mother now more than ever."

41

People have always said you shouldn't be angry with God, but I couldn't help it. "Why would you do something like this right now?" I'd shout at him.

I had a bachelor's of science degree from one of the top ten universities in the country in electrical engineering, but I couldn't change a diaper. I had only held one newborn and changed one diaper prior to having my own child. I never babysat children either. Isn't my mom supposed to teach me how to do this? Who is going to teach me now? Who is going to come and help me care for this newborn? Who am I going to send the kids to in the summer for a break? Who is going to spoil them and give them candy while I give them vegetables?

In the midst of all of this, I had to take my ten-day old son on an airplane. Aren't we supposed to wait a few months before taking babies to public places that can expose them to infections? I mean what can be more germ-infested than an airport? My son didn't even have all of his vaccinations yet. We had to get special permission to allow him to get on the plane that would take us to my mother's funeral.

The days leading up to the dreaded viewing were consumed with making arrangements for a flight, changing the baby, making funeral arrangements, sleeping only two to three hours at a time, packing, etc. I never once stopped and prayed. I was way too busy, angry, and tired for that. I knew I would be seeing the body of the strongest, most amazing woman I had ever known lying in a coffin void of all strength. I just didn't think I could handle that.

How do you prepare to say goodbye to someone who, at that very moment, you need the most? I did the only thing I knew how to do. I put on my clothes and my makeup. I got the baby dressed and my husband and I prepared to walk out the door.

"Before we leave," my husband said, "Let's pray."

"Pray? Are you serious? I'm too angry at God to pray." My husband was a pastor so this seemed to me to be one of his super-religious, Christian responses to crisis. Too worn out physically, mentally, and emotionally to argue, I agreed.

We got down on our knees together. He started praying. I can't say I remember his words. Then I prayed. Truthfully, I don't remember what I said either. But what I do remember is I cried a lot—no, I wailed a lot. I got caught up in a tornado of whirling emotions violently colliding together. But as the crying subsided and the praying concluded, the whirlwind stopped. It felt as though I had entered the eye of the storm where a strange sense of peace filled me. The Lord granted me this peace right there on the side of the bed in the middle of the worst storm I had ever experienced at that point in my life.

I heard the Lord say to me, "What you are about to see in that casket is not your mother. Your mother has a spirit that infused that body and made her who she was. Her spirit is in heaven with me. She is no longer in pain. When you see that body, you're seeing just a shell."

All of a sudden, strength came over me. I dried my tears and rose from my knees with a new outlook on my suffering. God didn't remove the pain and the hurt of losing my mother, but he did speak a peace that helped me to face the adversity at hand. That's the real purpose of prayer in the midst of your trials or adversity.

Prayer doesn't always change the problem, trial, or suffering; it changes you in the middle of your problem, trial, or suffering. Prayer doesn't always take away the anger, hurt, or pain; it helps you to deal with your anger, hurt, or pain.

I don't want to sugarcoat your trial or adversity and make you think that if you pray God will change everything for you. God is not about changing your circumstances as much as he is about changing you in your circumstances. With this in mind, we can see our trials in a more positive light. James 1:2-4 says, "Consider it pure joy, my brothers, whenever you face trials of many kinds." Before I continue, I know this Scripture seems crazy. You might be thinking right now, "I'm going through the most difficult adversities and trials I've ever known and you want me to consider that as joy? What joy is there in death? What joy is there in cancer? What joy is there in losing my job? What joy is there in losing my home? What joy can there possibly be in my adversity?"

If James stopped at "consider it pure joy when you face trials," it would not only seem crazy, it would make me mad. But he continues to tell us why we should see trials as joy: "Because you know that the testing of your faith develops perseverance. Perseverance must finish its work so that you may be mature and complete, not lacking anything" (James 1:3-4). God has a purpose for our trials—perseverance.

Unfortunately, we can't learn to persevere until we have been through situations that require us to keep moving forward in the midst of adversity. Perseverance helps us to grow up and become complete in the things of God. So, the real reason we should consider trials as joy is because God is transforming our character so that we will be mature and not lack anything.

When I think about it that way, I have joy and am grateful to God for every adversity. It's crazy but, looking back, I would not be the mom I am today without my mother's death. I would have been so dependent on her that I probably would not have learned to depend on God as my source during difficult times.

If it weren't for my husband forcing me to pray before my mom's funeral, I don't think I could have made it through that most trying time. Paul says in Ephesians 6:18: "Pray in the Spirit on all occasions with all kinds of prayers and requests." Prayer is one of the most overlooked pieces of offensive weapons in the middle of adversity, but praying is usually not our natural response. Sometimes we'll call a friend or try to figure out a solution on our own before we consider praying.

Just recently, I had to handle a difficult situation with one of my children. Not knowing what I should do, I picked up the phone and called a girlfriend, and then another. For two or three hours, I talked to as many people as I thought would listen. Talking to the last person, I was still in tears, upset, and angry. Then, in the middle of the conversation, my phone died. She tried to call me back but couldn't because her phone died as well. Finally, I realized, "Alright, Lord. Both phone lines are dead. I think I need to pray." Sometimes God puts us in a situation where all we can do is get on our knees and pray. When we're at the point when we don't know what to do, that's the time to pray.

So what *is* prayer? Prayer is simply our communication with God. Walter Wangerin in his book, *Whole Prayer*, identifies four parts of a circle of prayer: "First we speak, while second, God listens. Third God speaks, while fourth, we listen."[1] So we talk *with God*, not just *to God*. God talks with us, too, causing a circle to become whole between him and us (see Figure 2). Focusing on all four parts of the circle assures us that our conversation with God is just that—a conversation.

FIGURE 2: CIRCLE OF PRAYER

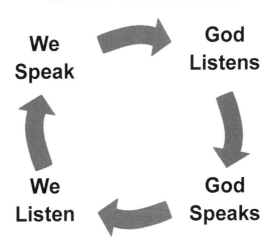

How do we pray when we're so angry, upset, and frustrated with God or others? Here are the keys that will unlock the practice of praying, even when we don't want to, so that we can have victory in adversity through conversations with God.

KEY 1: BE REAL AND HONEST WITH GOD

God desires truth from us in prayer, not perfect words. The religious, rote words we pray will not do anything for us during a trial. We can't pray, "Now I lay me down to sleep . . ." "Bless Mommy and Daddy . . ." "Our father which art in heaven . . ." No. We have to get real and tell God what is really in our heart.

We have to get so real that we lay all of our complaints on God as well. We have to say things like, "I'm sick of these children you gave me." "I'm ready to choke my wife and kill my boss." "I'm so much in grief that I can't take it no more and I'm ready to die!" The key to victory is *real* prayer. If we pray, "O Father, thou art holy and righteous . . ." but never share what is so heavy on our heart, we may as well not have prayed.

Instead of trying to sound perfect when talking with our Father, the apostle Peters says, "Cast all your anxiety on him because he cares for you" (1 Peter 5:7). God wants and waits for us to throw all of our anxiety, worry, fear, anger, and every thought or emotion on him during prayer. The reality is that some of the people we are closest to are the ones with whom we have been able to share our deepest feelings. God desires to be our best friend. That requires that we honestly share with him what is on our hearts. We can even ask him why this trial is happening to us.

Some people say we shouldn't ask God why we are suffering. I've never seen in the Bible where it says we can't ask God why. We do see that when Job went through difficult times and asked God why, God responded: "Where were you when I laid the foundation of the earth?" God told him off, but he didn't kill him. You see, God is all about us having a real relationship with him. If you are in a relationship with a friend and you can't ask, "Why did you do that?" what kind of relationship is it?

I ask God why all the time: "Why am I dealing with this? Why is my family going through this? Why God. why?" I have learned that I can ask God why, but he is not obligated to give me an answer. I have also learned that I must be okay with whatever answer he does provide. It may be that God will reveal a deep revelation as to why I'm going through this adversity. He may reveal my destiny and purpose in the middle of the trial, or God can simply let me know that he is transforming and maturing me so that I will become more complete, not lacking anything (James 1:2-4).

God can take whatever you throw at him in prayer. The best part is that he provides benefits to crying out to him in truth and honesty. Psalm 34:16-19 says,

> The eyes of the Lord are on the righteous and his ears are attentive to their cry....The righteous cry out, and the Lord hears them; he delivers them from all their troubles. The Lord is close to the brokenhearted and saves those who are crushed in spirit. A righteous man has many troubles, but the Lord delivers him from them all; he protects all his bones, not one of them will be broken.

When we cry out to God in prayer, he promises that he hears us and will deliver us from our troubles. Does that mean God will make the troubles go away the way we want them to? No, at least not every time. But it does mean that he promises in his own way at his own time to bring us out of our trouble. I've heard it said that "trouble don't last always" and that has been my experience, too.

KEY 2: DON'T STOP PRAYING

Praying one time during a trial is simply not enough. Just because we prayed yesterday and received peace and a breakthrough at the time, we must keep on praying. Three weeks after my mother died, I was so mad at God that I decided not to talk to him anymore. I hadn't prayed since I knelt on the side of the bed with my husband before the funeral service. Since that time, the emotional chaos returned. I felt consumed with grief at the loss of my mother; or maybe I was experiencing postpartum depression. It could have been both. It doesn't really matter. Suffice to say, I lived in horrible despair.

My husband said I should just tell God how angry I felt. I thought, "Hadn't I done that already? Do I really have to do it again?" He would tell me, "Just talk to God about how you feel? God is big enough to listen."

So I tried to pray again. The next time I nursed my newborn baby, I yelled at God at the same time. Praying on my knees was physically too difficult at that time, but I did pray in very unusual places at unusual times. I prayed in the morning, at night, in the car, while walking the baby, rocking the baby, and cooking dinner. The more I prayed, the less angry I felt. It got to the point that instead of *running from* God in prayer, the only way I could get through the day was to *run to* God in prayer.

If you're going to be victorious in your adversity, you can't stop praying. "Pray continually" as Paul wrote in 1 Thessalonians 5:17. Pray when you feel like it, and pray when you don't feel like it. Pray when it seems as though life is going well, and pray when everything is going wrong. Just keep on praying with all kinds of prayers and requests (Ephesians 6:18). Just keep talking to God through your trial. Something miraculous will occur. God will transform you in the midst of your prayer.

KEY 3: PRAY WITH THANKSGIVING

No matter how bad your adversity appears to be, you can find something to thank God about. Take a moment right now to make a list of twenty things you can be thankful for. You might say, "Nothing is going right; I have nothing to give thanks for." Yes, you do have some things to be thankful for. Here is a list to get you started. Depending on your situation, you might not be able to thank God for every item on this list, but it's a start that will hopefully jumpstart your own list of reasons to thank God.

Today I thank God:

1. For my salvation (Hebrews 7:25)
2. For forgiveness of sin (1 John 1:9)
3. That I am no longer condemned (Romans 8:1)
4. For breath in my body
5. For clothes on my back
6. For food on my table (It may not be steak and lobster, but thanks for beans and rice.)
7. For being in my right mind
8. For my family—no matter how amazing or crazy they are
9. For my friends
10. For strength to pray
11. For my health
12. For a place to lay my head at night
13. For my job
14. For my finances—(no matter how much or how little)
15. For God, who has always been good to me
16. For protection from dangers seen and unseen
17. For His grace
18. For His mercy
19. For His peace
20. For hope that tomorrow can and will be better than today

Excuse me for just a moment while I stop and give God all the praise and all the glory for all that he has done, is doing, and will continue to do in my life . . .

Somehow, when we pray with thanksgiving, it causes us to see God's goodness. Prayer with thanksgiving also leads us into worship. Worship is ascribing worth, honor, and glory to God through singing, shouting, dancing, lifting hands, clapping, or any other expression that glorifies God. Worship is the key to acknowledging that *he is God* and *we are not*. It keeps our focus straight. Worship is like a new pair of glasses through which we look at our trials and adversity. It reminds us of how he has always taken care of us and will continue to take care of us. It helps us to see how big God really is and how small our problem is in comparison to God.

Prayer with thanksgiving also leads us into true peace: "Do not be anxious about anything, but in everything, by prayer and petition, with thanksgiving, present your requests to God. And the peace of God, which transcends all understanding, will guard your hearts and your minds in Christ Jesus" (Philippians 4:6-7). As we pray with thanksgiving, God will grant us peace—not ordinary peace—a peace that transcends all human understanding.

KEY 4: PRAY WITH FAITH

When we pray in the midst of adversity, we must pray with an expectation that God is able to do exceedingly and abundantly above all that we ask, think, hope, or imagine (Ephesians 3:20). We must pray believing that God can do exactly what He said he would do in our situation. Without faith in God, we cannot please him (Hebrews 11:6). We'll talk more about faith in chapter 8. For now, pray with expectation.

What do we lose if we believe God will do a miracle or make a change for us? We might be disappointed when we don't receive what we're expecting when we're expecting it;

but with continuous expectation, we can have a sense of hope that life will get better. Therefore, a more profound question might be: "What will you lose if you don't believe?"

KEY 5: PRAY ALOUD

As we converse with God, we must not be silent. Too often, we pray only in our mind and not aloud. But the psalmist writes, "Evening and morning and at noon I will pray and cry aloud and He shall hear my voice" (Psalm 55:17 NKJV). Something about using our voice in prayer causes a release in us. How can we really scream and yell at God without even opening our mouths?

Find a comfortable, quiet spot where you can say whatever you need to say to God. Remember that Jesus prayed aloud in the Garden of Gethsemane where he was dealing with a tremendous adversity—he didn't want to go to the cross. The Bible says, "He fell with his face to the ground and prayed, 'My father, if it is possible may this cup be taken from me. Yet not as I will, but as you will'" (Matthew 26:39). Jesus prayed aloud as he spoke to the Father. We must also open our mouths and tell God what is on our heart.

In addition to praying with our hearts and minds, let me add a quick note on praying in the Spirit. There is power in praying aloud in our heavenly language. Jude says, "Dear friends, *build yourselves up* in your most holy faith and pray in the Holy Spirit" (Jude 20, italics added). We can encourage ourselves in the Lord when we pray in the Spirit.

Praying in the Spirit allows us to express what natural words cannot. Sometimes, we don't know what to say to God. These are the times to pray aloud in the Spirit. Paul explains this to the Christians in Rome when he writes,

The Spirit helps us in our weakness. We do not know what we ought to pray for, but the Spirit himself intercedes for us with groans that words cannot express. And he who searches our hearts knows the mind of the Spirit, because the Spirit intercedes for the saints in accordance with God's will (Romans 8:26-27).

When we're going through a difficult situation, we should pray even when we don't want to. It is while we are praying and talking with God (not just to God) that God will transform our heart, attitudes, thoughts, mind, will, and emotions. Prayer may not change the circumstances, but it definitely changes us.

CHAPTER 5

LIE YOUR WAY OUT
(Belt of Truth)

The Truth is heavy; therefore, few care to carry it.

~ Unknown

- The check is in the mail.
- I'll start my diet tomorrow.
- I'll pay you back when I get my check.
- Tell them I'm not at home.
- One size fits all.
- This hurts me more than it hurts you.
- I just need five minutes of your time.
- Open wide. It won't hurt a bit.
- Let's have lunch sometime.
- It's not the money; it's the principle.

Lying has become a part of our American culture. In fact, lying seems to be a way of life for many of us. We can lie at a moment's notice. The book, *The Day America Told the Truth*, says that

- 91 percent of people surveyed lie routinely about matters they consider trivial.

- 36 percent lie about important matters.

- 86 percent lie regularly to parents.

- 75 percent lie to friends.

- 73 percent lie to siblings.

- 69 percent lie to spouses.[2]

You may believe that you are in the minority of truth tellers; but when we go through adversity, one of our first responses is to lie. Here are some subtle ways we do this:

- We believe our divorce or separation is entirely our spouse's fault. We say things like, "He always . . ." and "She never . . ." But in reality, *always* and *never* are rarely true.

- We believe our ailing health is God's fault, instead of facing the truth that maybe we didn't care for our bodies like God wants us to.

- We believe that when our children struggle with drugs or alcohol, it's not our fault. We fail to admit that each time they have seen us high or drunk, it may have contributed to our children's addictive behaviors.

On July 11, 2007, I had to face a difficult situation that I lied about for years. Early that morning, I slipped walking down the stairs, belting out a scream that woke up everyone in the house. I heard the crack and knew that I had broken my ankle. I just didn't know how badly. My husband took the kids to school and then took me to the hospital. The doctor said it was the worst break he had ever seen—two bones broken in five different places. That night, after emergency surgery, I became confined to crutches and a wheelchair. A non-walking cast covered my ankle for three months and to make matters worse, I was a mother of two small boys and couldn't drive.

So where does the lie come in? I believed the fall was just an accident. I didn't want to admit that my leg and ankle muscles were weak from lack of exercise and poor diet. I had reached the highest weight in my life, yet I blamed the carpet, the stairs, the devil—everything but myself. The truth was that my body wasn't strong enough to handle its own weight, but I kept lying to myself that I could keep eating whatever I wanted and not have to deal with any repercussions.

Whether the lies we tell in the middle of adversity are directed to others or to ourselves, they're still lies that fuel our adversity. Paul encourages believers to "stand firm then, with the belt of truth buckled around your waist" (Ephesians 6:14).

This belt refers to part of a Roman soldier's armor. It was designed for three strategic purposes: (1) as a leather apron that hung under the metal protecting the soldier's thighs, (2) as a belt to hold his clothes and sword secure during battle, and (3) as a guard for his most private and precious components. Truth serves to protect us, provide security, and cover what is precious in our lives. The belt of truth, then, is designed to help us live a life of integrity during adversity.

While in the wheelchair for three months, I had time to really reflect on the lies I was believing. One early morning during prayer, the Lord spoke the truth to me: "The devil is trying to kill you and you keep allowing him access."

"What? The devil wants me dead!?"

I sat in disbelief, not knowing what to say or think. God then reminded me that he had a purpose and a plan for my life, and the enemy did not want to see that plan come to fruition. Although that bothered me, I was more appalled that I had been allowing Satan an opportunity to kill me.

God also reminded me of the story of Job in the Old Testament. In the book of Job, Satan and God have a conversation about Job. Satan is looking for someone to bother, even devour, and God asks him if he has considered God's servant, Job. God shares with Satan that Job is upright and blameless and fears the Lord. God is virtually volunteering Job for severe trial and adversity. God will often volunteer us to go through suffering because he just wants to show us, and a dying world, what is in our character.

As the story continues, Satan says, "Have you put a hedge around him and his household and everything he has?" (Job 1:10). He was telling God that he couldn't touch Job because there is a hedge of protection around him. I realized at that moment that God had placed a hedge of protection around me. However, every time I ate poorly, did not exercise, lied about the awful condition of my body, I left an opening in my hedge of protection, which Satan used to enter and attack. *God was trying to protect me, but I was leaving the gate open.* God placed a belt of truth around me concerning Satan's plan for my life and my participation in it.

You will never gain victory if you continue to be dishonest with others or with yourself. God already knows the truth, you might as well agree with him and acknowledge the truth, too. Bob Harris discovered this in the most difficult way. Journalist, Nancy Shullins, writes the following true story:

> Bob Harris, weatherman for NY TV station WPIX-TV and the nationally syndicated independent Network news, had to weather a public storm of his own making in 1979. Though he had studied math, physics and geology at three colleges, he left school without a degree but with a strong desire to be a media weatherman. He phoned WCBS-TV, introducing himself as a Ph.D. in geophysics from Columbia U. The phony degree got him in the door. After a two-month tryout, he was hired as an off-camera forecaster for WCBS. For the next decade his career flourished. He became widely known as "Dr. Bob." He was also hired by the *New York Times* as a consulting meteorologist. The same year both the Long Island Railroad and then Baseball Commissioner Bowie Kuhn hired him.
>
> Forty years of age and living his childhood dream, he found himself in public disgrace and national humiliation when an anonymous letter prompted WCBS management to investigate his academic credentials. Both the station and the *New York Times* fired him. His story got attention across the land. He was on the Today Show, the Tomorrow Show, and in *People Weekly*, among others. He thought he'd lose his home and never work in the media again. Several days later the Long Island Railroad and Bowie Kuhn announced they would not fire him. Then WNEW-TV gave him a job. He admits it

was a dreadful mistake on his part and doubtless played a role in his divorce. "I took a shortcut that turned out to be the long way around, and one day the bill came due. I will be sorry as long as I am alive." [3]

Real integrity is who we are when no one is looking. It's the truth about what we've done and what we really desire in any situation. Integrity is truth in the inmost part of our being.

Maintaining integrity during a trial comes from the discipline to maintain integrity before the trial. It's like a soldier who, during boot camp, learns discipline, obedience, and integrity so that when the real war begins, these new or strengthened character traits will be second nature. Likewise, once we have practiced the discipline of walking in truth before God, ourselves, and others during peaceful times, it will become our second nature during adversity. We can bury the lying, cheating, and stealing with our former character and give birth to a new integrity.

Many people in the Bible relied on a high level of integrity to help them overcome their adversities. Joseph in the book of Genesis chapter 39 is one example. Joseph had a master whose wife wanted him to sleep with her. What is the natural desire of a man in this situation? What about a slave? Joseph had to decide which of his desires would prevail: lust of his flesh or loyalty to his master. Joseph chose not to dishonor his master by committing this sin of adultery. His master's wife became so enraged at his rejection that she accused Joseph of raping her.

The charge against him was false, but Joseph decided that being true to his values and going to prison anyway was far better than lying to his master, committing adultery, and remaining a free man. Although imprisoned, Joseph could sleep at night because he did the right thing. Integrity does not always mean that we won't go through trials; it means that we'll be able to look at ourselves in the mirror each day and know that we did not compromise our values in order to get out of trouble.

Joseph reacted with such strength of character because he had already set his standard of integrity before the lustful temptation began. If he had not done so, it might have been quite easy for him to give into the seductive advances and cover up the affair with lies. Likewise, when we have not set certain standards in our lives, it's easy to accept whatever solutions the world offers us. Predetermine today what you will do during such trials so that you won't give in to any temptations that will damage your integrity. This is especially important for singles trying to maintain celibacy.

As a widow, I have predetermined healthy boundaries with the opposite sex. If I don't establish such standards and decide now what I can and cannot do, I just might choose to give in to the desire of lust. I can't let myself be tempted like that again. I have learned that lust without boundaries creates desperation to fulfill it. Without boundaries, I will walk across lines that I have not yet drawn. For instance, I might meet with an attractive man alone and that will likely lead to sex and that will likely lead to a lot of pain. In the end, desperation often leads to destruction—emotional, physical, and even financial.

Setting boundaries is the reason budgets are so powerful. A budget is simply a predetermined plan for how I will spend my money. In the middle of a crisis or temptation, I don't spend money on something outside of the budget because there is already a plan for where every dollar will go. When

a bill comes up that is not in the budget, I don't stress. If I
don't have the money, then I just don't have the money.

If I go shopping and see a fabulous pair of shoes that
goes perfectly with the stunning dress that I have yet to
buy, I say to myself, "No. My money has been predetermined
to go somewhere else." When I shop with money set aside
for a specific purpose, all of the guilt and desperation to
buy other stuff disappears. This keeps the integrity of my
budget intact because I don't desperately desire something
I can't afford.

Maintaining our integrity with the help of Jesus *who
is truth and integrity* helps us to determine who we really
belong to. We do have a choice. Jesus told the Jews who did
not believe in him,

> You belong to your father, the devil, and you want
> to carry out your father's desire. He was a murderer
> from the beginning, not holding to the truth, for there
> is no truth in him. When he lies, he speaks his na-
> tive language, for he is a liar and the father of lies
> (John 8:44).

The desire to know the truth and speak the truth during adversity reveals that we truly belong to God. However,
when we choose to speak lies or believe a lie, we fulfill Satan's
perfect plan for our life.

If asked, "Would you rather feel good while believing a
lie or suffer while knowing the truth," I think most people
would prefer to feel good. What about you? What's your
choice today? When adversity strikes, will you choose to
lie your way out? Or will you pick up the belt of truth and
maintain your integrity?

CHAPTER 6

DEALING WITH
A BROKEN HEART
(Breastplate of Righteousness)

The heart is the only broken instrument that works.

\- T. E. Kalem

The rejection, loneliness, and loss of love was able. My first thought was not to pray, call a friend, reach out for help, or even believe that God had a better plan. No. The love of my life said he didn't want to be with me anymore and, in that moment, I wanted to go to sleep and never wake up again.

At age nineteen, I had no hope left. There was no way things would ever get better. "Why should I face tomorrow when it's only going to be as painful as today?" I thought. So I started planning how I would leave this world: "I don't feel strong enough to hang myself. I have no access to a gun to shoot myself. Maybe, I should pop a bottle of pills." But alas, no. Those humdrum suicide headlines had already been written. Instead, I walked outside late at night in the dead of a Chicago winter and laid myself down in the middle of the street, hoping a car would run me over.

Icing up on the snow-covered asphalt, I wondered if this is what it would feel like to be dead, to lie there cold, unmoving, and helpless. I wondered about how my family would feel once they heard the news. What I remember most is thinking: "I hope my ex-boyfriend will feel guilty for leaving me. Maybe this pain will get back at him for all the pain he's caused me." It all felt really strange and twisted to me, but that's what kept running through my mind.

While listening attentively for a fast-approaching car, I had nowhere to look but up—up at a universe of brightness beyond my own dark and dreary neighborhood—a world so much grander than the one I knew. Pondering this greatness, I heard something, like a whisper touch my heart: "I have so much more for you."

"What? Did I hear really that? No. C'mon. If this is you, God, my life is never going to be okay again. There's no way out of this one."

"I have so much more for you," came the whisper again.

Instantly, I saw myself sitting in church a year earlier where I heard a similar voice: "I have something big for you to do. Will you do it?"

I thought I might be crazy. After all, who hears words in their head? So I just cried. But now, waiting to die, I sensed those same words again: "I have something big for you to do. Will you do it?" This time, I knew God was revealing himself to me. God, the creator of this great universe had a plan for my life.

Shuddering in the cold, I knew that it was God who allowed me to keep breathing. Each exhale released a seed of hope—the hope that God would fulfill his promises and his plans for my future. I also knew that the only way this hope could be taken away from me is if *I chose* to take away my last breath.

I whispered back with renewed hope and love, "Yes, Lord. I'll do it," and I ran back into the house.

To this day, I don't know what "it" is, but I do know that God's plan is not to harm me or to destroy me. His plan is to give me a hope and a future (Jeremiah 29:11). That's a promise, so I just keep obeying and believing God that he is going to do something "big" with my life.

I now see that when God plans out a life, Satan cannot stop it. However, the enemy can and often does get us to doubt and even destroy our belief that God is able to change our lives. He does this by messing with our heart and mind so that we end up feeling hopeless about ourselves and helpless in our situation.

Satan is so smart. He knows that we like to react according to our feelings and emotions. He knows that human nature says, "If it feels good do it" and "If it feels bad do nothing." Doing nothing, though, cripples us. It causes some of us to lie prostrate on a residential road in the dead of winter hoping for a car to smash us flat.

Our emotions really do fuel our actions. That's why it's so important to protect them when we go through a difficult situation. I don't mean to stop feeling. That wouldn't be healthy. But to be victorious during adversity, we must guard our emotions by protecting our heart and finding a safe, healthy environment to release those feelings.

Proverbs 4:23 says, "Above all else guard your heart for it is the wellspring of life." The heart in this text doesn't just refer to the organ in our chest; it refers to our mind and the whole personality of a person. Our capacity to live life with joy and passion comes from within our whole being, not from outside circumstances.

This capacity to live with joy and passion is our "wellspring of life." So in order to have peace, passion, and joy during difficult life issues, we must guard what comes into our hearts, mind, and soul. We must protect our wellspring of life from those who will hurt or abuse it.

Paul tells us how to do this in Ephesians 6 when he says to put on the "breastplate of righteousness." A breastplate protects a soldier's most vital organs, such as the heart, lungs, liver, and stomach. Any blow suffered to these vital areas could be deadly. In the spiritual realm, whenever we experience tragic events, the breastplate covers deadly blows of despair, hopelessness, and worthlessness that could cause us to completely break down and, like me, attempt suicide.

Guarding our heart is not the same as building a wall around it. Walls keep others out and lock ourselves in. A wall denies access to the people who need to be in our close, emotional circle. Without them, we hinder our learning, growing, and maturing.

Let's examine three keys that, if used, will guard your heart and emotions in the middle of an adversity without building walls.

KEY 1: ALLOW YOURSELF TO FEEL WHATEVER YOU FEEL

During difficult situations, many of us feel pain so intensely that we either think we can't continue living or else we push the pain aside and feel nothing at all. But neither extreme is healthy. It's alright to feel whatever emotion you feel when you feel it. We must allow ourselves to cry, shout, be angry, hit a punching bag, or whatever it takes to release the pain. Of course, we need to find a way to release these emotions so that no one gets hurt. But the bottom line is that bottled up emotions are toxic.

Not allowing ourselves the time or space to feel what's in our heart will cause us to mask it in unhealthy ways. We might self-medicate, withdraw, immerse ourselves in work, or become emotionally unavailable. We might create a self-condemning conversation in our head and begin to feel completely unworthy and insecure. We might feel as though we will never be forgiven or that we can never forgive. We might think that our family or friends will never forgive us even if God does. Masking emotions leads to severe depression and hopelessness.

Unfortunately, many of us don't know how to unmask our feelings because we grew up in homes where we were taught, through verbal and non-verbal communication, not to share them. Maybe as a child, we shared our anger and got punished or ridiculed for it. Perhaps we cried over a lost toy and were scorned for showing "weakness." As a result, we pretend we have no feelings. We tell others that nothing is wrong. We believe that even if something is wrong, we shouldn't talk about it. We figure out a way to handle it ourselves.

My father, for example, was an alcoholic who physically and verbally beat my mother. In my early years, I watched him stab her with a knife, beat her on our front lawn, and curse her out almost weekly, just to mention a few incidents. I saw my mother wear turtlenecks in the middle of a Midwest summer to cover the bruises and scratch marks on her neck where my father tried to strangle her the night before. I watched her wake up, go to work, and take care of us kids every day like nothing was wrong.

She never told us not to talk about it, it's just that *she* never talked about it. Based on her example, I learned that when tragedy strikes, I need to get up the next day and go to work like nothing happened. I learned not to tell anyone how I really felt or about what happened the night before.

If my mother had put on the breastplate of righteousness and guarded her heart, she would have found a safe place where she could release the hurt locked up inside. We need to do the same. The safest place or person we can turn to is God, who certainly isn't afraid to hear exactly how we feel. The blessing for this honesty is that God promises to meet us at our deepest place of hurt, right where we are. He doesn't require that we become emotionally stable to talk to him. As a matter of fact, he wants us to come to him broken, hurting, and dejected. Jesus says, "It is not the healthy who need a doctor, but the sick. I have not come to call the righteous, but sinners" (Mark 2:17).

No matter what situation we face; whether it's the loss of a loved one, the loss of a job, problems with your family, or loss of finances, there is no textbook way to handle it. God just wants us to be real and open with him and ourselves about what we're feeling so that healing can truly begin to take place.

God should be the first person we talk to in a tragedy. He is a safe place, where we can blow up, yell, scream, cry, or do whatever we need to do in order to release the pain in our hearts. When my husband died, I needed a safe place to cry. I was a single parent with two little boys, ages five and two. I was the senior pastor of a grieving church and a community leader of grieving youth. I talked, cried, and screamed at God a lot. My wellspring of life became a geyser of tears I could not contain. They simply gushed out of me, even at inappropriate moments (at the mall or holiday celebrations). During this time, I needed to guard my heart and make sure that I had a safe environment to release the emotions to a trusted friend. This leads me to the second key to guarding our heart in the middle of adversity.

KEY 2: SURROUND YOURSELF WITH PEOPLE YOU TRUST

Imagine shaking a full bottle of soda with the cap tightly secured. The bubbles build up and, if allowed to escape, erupt all over the place making a mess. During adversity, we are like the soda. We have been shaken uncontrollably. If we don't have people around us who can be our cap of protection, we can explode and make messes out of our lives.

The death of my husband in October of 2008 from a massive heart attack violently shook my world on every level. We had founded a church and a nonprofit organization together. My husband served as the senior pastor of that church and the executive director of the organization. In one day, I assumed the responsibility of a church that needed guidance, financial decisions that needed to be made, a nonprofit that needed direction, and two young boys that needed a strong, loving parent.

Relying on trusted family, friends, a great Christian therapist, and spiritual guidance allowed my heart to bubble over in a safe place. My older brother, especially, provided invaluable protection. He made sure that people who would not understand my pain and who tried to press their own agendas during this time were far removed from me. He took care of situations for me that I could not emotionally handle.

He helped me to determine what activities were healthy to be involved with and which ones were not.

Working with a pastor or Christian counselor during a trial is important, but the relationships we need in a crisis won't always be developed in the midst of the trial. Many times, they come from people with whom we have invested significant time, energy, and trust. It's especially helpful to nurture healthy relationships with believers inside the church before a trial so that when we need to release emotionally, they will be available to provide encouragement, just as Hebrews 10:25 advises, "Let us not give up meeting together, as some are in the habit of doing, but let us encourage one another—and all the more as you see the Day approaching."

I relied on the support of a Christian brother during the viewing of my husband's body. I knew that the service the next day would be very public and a lot of people would be in attendance, but I didn't want to deal with them at this moment. I didn't want them watching me and the children in our distress, either. I just wanted time for my sons and I to say goodbye in private, so I asked one of our deacons to clear the room so that we could grieve privately. He received a lot of negative feedback and heartache for that. More importantly, though, my sons and I were able to grieve the way we wanted and needed to because he became a shield for us.

This kind of shield and support is available to you in a variety of people and circumstances. When in the midst of adversity, don't hesitate to allow trusted friends to answer your phone when you really don't want to be bothered. Allow them to talk to a loved one on your behalf when your relationship with them is struggling. Allow them to handle details of difficult situations so that you don't have to. Allow them to take your children to the park when you really need a break. Allow them to bless you financially when you're in a severe financial crisis. Allow them to be your heart's shield as needed.

KEY 3: TRUST IN THE LORD TO BE YOUR SHIELD

> Praise be to the Lord,
>   for he has heard my cry for mercy.
> The Lord is my strength and my shield;
>   my heart trusts in him, and I am helped
> My heart leaps for joy
> And I will give thanks to him in song.
>   ~ Psalms 28:6-7

The Lord is our strength and our shield. When our heart trusts in him, he helps us. So let's trust him with our emotions and feelings. Trust him with aches and pains. Trust him with worries and frustrations. When we trust God and cry out to him, something begins to happen. He not only acts as a shield, he increases our strength and causes our heart to leap for joy.

Trusting God with our heart also means that we learn to worship him in the midst of our emotions. God desires that we worship him in good times and in bad times: I may be on my knees crying, but I am still able to declare that the Lord is good because I have knees that are able to bend. I may have lost a loved one, but I am still able to worship God because I will see my loved one again in heaven. I may be depressed and feeling completely hopeless, but I am able to praise God because he works all things for my good. No matter what we are going through, if we trust God with our heart and praise him, it will change everything.

When we trust God with our emotions, it doesn't have to be with a smile, clap, or a dance. We just have to pour our heart out to him. Believe it or not, it's even alright to be angry with God and still worship him. This might sound something like, "Lord, I am angry that my child has died, but you are still God who is in control. I worship you because you are the sovereign Lord, and I trust you."

Another powerful emotion we have to hand over to God is fear. Fear is the place where we are the most vulnerable during a trial. It is the place where the enemy tries to cause us to spend the most time. Why? Any time Satan causes our hearts to fear, he can exploit it to try to destroy us. If we get afraid enough, he knows we'll become immobilized. As a matter of fact, fear is the opposite of faith. Anytime we operate in fear we do not have faith. How does Satan work to get us to fear? He looks at the videotape of our life and identifies the places where he knows we're afraid. Then he tries to force us to go to those same places in our minds.

But we can fight back. We can adopt the position of Psalm 27:3, which says, "Though an army besiege me, my heart will not fear; though war break out against me, even then will I be confident." Don't be afraid to stand firm and be confident in the word of God. If you have fear in your heart, research the Scriptures and find words that will infuse you with faith. Every time you think that you are afraid, speak the word of God and recite those Scriptures until the fear is vanished away (see chapter 10 for how to pray the Scriptures).

To prevent a breakdown or to rise out of a place where you feel completely broken, guard your heart and emotions.

Find trusted counselors, advisors, and friends to talk to. And let God be your ultimate shield of your heart. The heart is a vital organ and so is the mind. To have peace in adversity, we need to guard both. In the next chapter, we'll learn how to protect our mind with the helmet of salvation.

CHAPTER 7

THE WAR FOR
PEACE OF MIND
(Gospel of Peace)

*Peace is not the absence of conflict,
it is the ability to handle conflict by peaceful means.*

- Ronald Reagan

Have you ever wondered how some Christians seem to have it all together during a death, a bankruptcy, or a divorce? Why don't they fall apart like the rest of us? Is it a gene they inherited at conception? Did they take a class at church to learn it? Is it just a part of their personality?

The answer is yes and no. The good news is that if peace is not inherent in our personality, it can be learned and put into practice at critical moments so that we will see a breakthrough when we would otherwise experience a breakdown.

We cannot control the outside forces that affect our lives such as other people, the economy, or death. God doesn't always remove the storms from our lives, either, but he does want to give us peace in the midst of them. He even shows us how to walk in peace in the middle of trying times—and that ability is a powerful weapon against the enemy.

It can feel like winning the lottery, but peace doesn't need to be so rare. Let's examine three keys to unlocking the doors to peace in the midst of adversity.

KEY 1: MAKE THE RECIPE FOR PEACE

Quietness, tranquility, free from disturbance or worry—that's peace. It seems so simple to say: "Have peace" and we know that God wants us to have peace, so how do we do that? How can we make peace for ourselves when we're utterly worried, frustrated, afraid, or angry?

The answer lies in a recipe. Recipes are fantastic because if we follow them correctly, we should end with a consistent result every time. The recipe for the peace we need during adversity is found in Philippians 4:6-7: "Do not be anxious about anything, but in everything, by prayer and petition, with thanksgiving, present your requests to God. And the peace of God, which transcends all understanding, will guard your hearts and your minds in Christ Jesus." Therefore, the recipe for peace is

    1 cup of prayer
    ½ cup of petitions in prayer
    5 cups of thanksgiving

    Sift out anxiety and worry. Mix prayer, requests, and thanksgiving. Preheat the prayer room oven with worship until the temperature reaches 370 degrees. Bake recipe in the prayer room for a minimum of 15 minutes or until you feel the peace rising inside. Note: Longer

times in the oven may be required for extremely difficult days. Reheat the mixture as necessary throughout
the day.

If you follow this recipe, peace will supernaturally over-
take you. You will not understand or be able to explain it
because this peace surpasses all human understanding.
Let's look closer at how to make peace.

SIFT OUT ANXIETY AND WORRY.

The first part of this recipe calls for sifting out anxiety and
worry. Typically, we experience uneasiness, fear, nagging
concern, or apprehension as we consider the possible negative outcomes of our difficult situation. We worry about the
"what ifs." We process in our minds questions, like "What
if I die from this disease?" "What if my spouse leaves me?"
"What if I have cancer?" "What if I lose my job?"

The reality is that "what ifs" will cause us to worry about
a situation that we may or may not ever have to deal with.
This type of worry and anxiety is a drain on our time and
mental energy. Time is a precious gift of God and, yet, we
give it away for free to the enemy when we worry.

MIX PRAYER, REQUESTS, AND THANKSGIVING.

The best way to sift out anxiety and worry is to cast them
onto God (1 Peter 5:7). How? Every time we let our minds
consider a "what if," we need to pray to God, telling him
about our worry, fears, and anxiety. We need to let him
know why, at this precise moment, we are so concerned.
Casting our worries onto God is all about giving him our
prayer request and asking him to handle the situation for

us. It is literally throwing our problems onto God and getting them off of us.

As we pray, it's important to not only make requests and petitions to God, but to mix in a heap of thanksgiving and praise. Thanksgiving causes us to acknowledge what God has already done and to be encouraged that he is able to help us again. We should never overlook the good things that God has already provided for us, especially the precious gift of his Son, Jesus. Our salvation in Christ is so precious because no matter how bad things get, even to the point of death, at least we know we'll be with Christ in eternity with no more pain, sorrow, or tears.

Peace on earth requires making a conscious choice to cast our cares on God and dismiss the "what ifs." In other words, we have to disregard these thoughts and demand that our mind choose to pray and give God thanks instead. We must begin to train our minds to make the exchange. The best way to be anxious about nothing is to pray about everything.

The reality is that when we apply the recipe for peace, it markedly increases our faith and ability to trust God. It shows that we're confident that God is able to take care of us. If God can feed the birds and clothe the lilies of the field, how much more will he care for us (Matthew 6:25-34). God already knows our needs; however, when we talk to God about them and cast our cares on him, we demonstrate our dependence on God.

In chapter 4, I wrote about being vulnerable before God. As we pray and make our requests known to God, it's also best to be specific. We need to tell God exactly what we are requesting of him. For example, if we need a financial breakthrough, don't just say, "Lord, bless me financially." Tell him exactly how much money you need. It's important because Jesus gives us a promise that if we remain in him and his word remain in us, we can ask whatever we wish and it will be given to us (John 15:7).

Although we are able to make requests to God, our peace does not come from receiving the request. Our peace comes from releasing our request and our need to God and trusting that he is in control of our situation. God is not obligated to say yes to every request, but he does always answer the prayer in one of three ways: *yes, no* or *yes, but not now*.

Make sure that your peace does not rest in God answering your prayer the way you want when you want. If that is your goal, you might never receive real peace. This is for your best interest because you and I often make requests that aren't perfectly in line with the will of God. This is why I love God so much. I can ask him for anything. I can talk to him about whatever I'm worried or fearful about. I don't have to sift through my requests to find those that match the will of God.

When we feel anxious, all we have to do is make the request and trust him. If it's his will, he will fulfill our request; and if it's not, that's alright as well. He will still take care of us. It's not our job to worry about whether the prayer request is right in his eyes or not; we just need to make our request known to God with thanksgiving.

After my husband died, the worry about finances, the boys, the ministry, our home, and the organization overwhelmed me. But instead of thinking about how bad the outcome would be, I got on my knees and just prayed to God. I worshipped and thanked him because I trusted that he would always provide.

I remember the night he passed. After crying and praying with my children, they finally went to sleep. I came downstairs to cry out to God by myself. I talked to him for the rest of the night until the boys woke up crying the next morning. I cried so much and prayed so much that I truly had nothing left to say. I just moaned before God every night for two weeks after his death. When the morning arrived, I would still be in tears, but I had peace. The peace was a confidence and a hope that I knew that with Christ everything would be okay. Even though I was still crying, God granted me peace in the midst of my storm.

Once we utilize the recipe for peace, we receive a promise from God that we shall have peace that will guard our heart and mind in Christ Jesus.

KEY 2: TRAIN YOUR MIND FOR PEACE

As discussed in the previous chapter, Satan targets our weak points, physically and spiritually. For example, it would likely take a miracle of God to survive a gunshot to the brain. In the spiritual realm, the mind is also a critical and vulnerable organ (so is the heart).

Satan knows this and targets it. Real peace, then, provides a shield around our mind (and heart) to keep us from the need to worry about any further attacks from the enemy. Satan can take his best shot; but if we have the peace of God that transcends all understanding, we can live securely in God's divine protection. This is why we have been assured that no weapon that comes against us will prosper (Isaiah 54:17).

Real peace fills us when we train our minds to focus on God in the middle of our trials. If we train the mind enough, we will have disciplined it in such a way that every time we feel anxious or worried, we'll automatically put the recipe into action and peace will result. Isaiah 26:3 says, "You will keep in perfect peace him whose mind is steadfast, because he trusts in you."

In Hebrew, "steadfast" means to lean, lay, rest, support, put, uphold, or lean upon. So the way we nurture a peaceful mind is to rest in and lean on God because we have full confidence in him. A peaceful mind is upheld by God because he is trustworthy.

Resting our mind on God means that we constantly think godly thoughts and ideas. We think about what is true, noble, right, pure, lovely, admirable, excellent, or praiseworthy (Philippians 4:8). We must saturate our minds with the knowledge and character of God. Our minds should be thinking on a higher plane than our meager situations.

Unfortunately, peace doesn't come without a fight. It requires that we stay focused on the good things of God and not on the bad things of the world. I have trained my mind in this way. In the midst of adversity, I'm able to focus on God and not on my own feelings, emotions, or thoughts. The more I've done this, the easier it is to do again.

During the time following my husband's death, I certainly felt worried and anxious. However, to keep from going crazy, I played worship music in the house. I continued to read my Bible even when I didn't feel like it. And when it became too difficult to read the word, I listened to preachers on TV, CD, internet, or the radio. I made sure that either the word of God or godly music constantly surrounded me during this difficult time.

I encourage you to make a playlist of your favorite Christian music and let it fill your mind in the car and at home. Turn the television off; watching the pain and pleasures of the world will make you depressed. There's nothing worse than feeling defeated, broken, and alone during your adversity, so take charge of your mind and keep anything that is not of God out of it. Focus on him—focus on the positive.

Keeping our mind focused on God when we're so very tired is easier said than done. Some of us are trying to find another job or looking for a second job. We're traveling back and forth between hospitals. We're making arrangements for funerals and guests. We're so tired at the end of the day that we turn on the television, radio, or computer to lull us into a state of forgetfulness. We think it will only be for thirty minutes, but we get so engrossed that we fall asleep extremely late, making us even more tired when we awaken the next day.

Sometimes, in order to keep our minds focused on God during the day, we simply need to get some old-fashioned rest the night before. A hot bath, listening to worship music, and lying down afterward relaxes my mind enough to make me sleepy so that I can get a good night's rest. I wake up in the morning with enough alertness to focus my mind on God.

What positive ways cause you to relax and unwind so that you can get a good night's sleep?

KEY #3: LIVE AT PEACE WITH EVERYONE

Some of the ugliest and most bitter battles between people occur during severe trials and adversity. This is natural but Paul says, "As far as it depends on you, live at peace with everyone" (Romans 12:17). This unnatural, final key to experiencing peace—living at peace with everyone even in the storm— is the most difficult. Funerals, for example, often cause a difficult time to become extremely trying, not because we have lost a loved one but because we also have to deal with the loved ones who are still alive.

The Bible prescribes how to live at peace during tumultuous times. Based on Romans 12:14-21, here is how God wants us to live at peace with others during a storm. But wait. You might need to take a chill pill first and swallow it whole because this prescription is not easy. Trust me.

Okay, let's begin:

1. BLESS (AND DO NOT CURSE) THOSE WHO PERSECUTE YOU

The word "bless" means to speak well of. I can't dismiss the difficulty of speaking well of someone who has caused us pain. It's truly a challenge. But one reason we don't have peace is because of the anger we harbor against those who have hurt us. We want so much to speak negatively about them that not allowing it to come out of our mouth is extremely difficult. The truth is that the more we talk negatively about someone, the angrier we get. So speaking well of them or not speaking of them at all will help us keep peace in our heart.

What if someone is hurling raging insults at us? If you're like me, my first thoughts are not, "How can I speak well of them." Instead, I'm sifting through my mental dictionary of street lingo to make my point on their crude level. However, now that I'm a mother, I know that what my mother said so many times is godly advice: "If you don't have anything nice to say, don't say anything at all."

On our own effort, we can't hold our tongue *and* bless those who persecute us. But in our time of prayer, after we have released all of our negative thoughts to God, we often find the strength to pray that God would bless those who hurt us and allow us to do the same.

Okay, this one may be too hard. Let's go to the next one.

2. DO NOT REPAY EVIL FOR EVIL

At some point, we'll want to return fire at someone who has launched missiles of pain at us. But we have to leave the vengeance to God. God will take care of those who have hurt us. There's no pain we can do to someone that can ever come close to the pain that God can inflict on them. So why not leave the situation to God to handle for you? As Paul says, "Do not take revenge, my friends, but leave room for God's wrath, for it is written: 'It is mine to avenge; I will repay says the Lord'" (Romans12:19).

3. BE CAREFUL TO DO WHAT IS RIGHT IN THE EYES
    OF EVERYONE.

You may not be able to please everyone, but at least try to do what seems to be the right thing in your difficult situation. This is a sure-fire way to make your enemies upset and it's biblical. If your enemies are hungry, feed them; if they are thirsty, give them something to drink.

When we do these acts of kindness, it's like pouring hot coals all over their head (Romans 12:20). I absolutely love this Scripture. It means that while I am obeying God and treating my enemies nice, I am burning them up at the same time. I love God's Word!

The bottom line for living in peace with others is to bless those who hurt us and trust God to handle the rest.

Peace is often hardest to find in the midst of a storm. However, if you use the recipe for peace and focus on living at peace with others it will be easier to walk in peace when life is just going crazy.

CHAPTER 8

FAITH THAT WON'T QUIT
(Shield of Faith)

Faith is taking the first step
even when you don't see the whole staircase.

- Rev. Dr. Martin Luther King, Jr.

We sat in the small fishing boat slightly excited about what was about to happen and deathly afraid of what was happening, especially the uncontrolled shaking and rocking. There, off the shore of Waikiki in Hawaii, my husband and I prepared to parasail for the first time, even in the midst of a storm. I remembered that I couldn't swim and wondered how we would make it safely back to land, let alone soar three hundred feet in the air with the winds raging and rain pouring.

It's one thing to be in a storm on land but quite another to be in a storm in the ocean. Scratch that. It's worse to be in a storm three hundred feet in the air attached to a small fishing boat by a single cord. At least on land, you can hold on to something that seems stable and pray that the wind won't blow you away.

Because we paid for this adventure, my husband and I decided to stay with it. The guide strapped parachutes on our backs and, in a flash, we were whisked into the sky. I could feel the gusts of wind as we ascended, but it didn't seem as threatening as the chaotic sea so far below. In the air, I no longer felt afraid. I even forget about the storm as I focused on the beautiful Hawaiian coastline and gorgeous, deep blue water that now appeared so calm.

This controlled, yet free-floating flight gave me a deeper understanding of my faith, which is to say, my confidence in God. I trust God, now, in the same way I trusted the parachute on my back when I parasailed. The more I trust and believe God's word, the higher up he takes me. He causes me to see the beauty amidst the storm, not the tragedy. The higher I go, the more I'm able to lose sight of the enormity of my circumstances and focus on the enormity of my God.

As the guide slowly reeled in the cord, we returned to the turbulent sea and the rocking boat. Likewise, when I lose my faith, I quickly get reeled back in to my problems. Situations that once looked like harmless ants become mountains of turmoil.

Paul knew this to be true, so in addition to guarding our hearts with the breastplate of righteousness, Paul says in Ephesians 6 that we need to also wear the shield of faith. The purpose of the shield of faith is to deflect the flaming arrows of fear, depression, doubt, and worry in our lives. The only time that Satan's arrows can hit us is if our shield is down—when we stop believing that God is working things out for our good. We keep our shield up by standing behind our faith in God and in his word.

Faith is having complete trust and confidence in God no matter the circumstance. It is the ability to believe in what we cannot see and still act on God's word for our lives. Faith takes action on God's word by leaving the results to God.

Real faith is not just about believing in God; it's about trusting God's word and moving out to obey him regardless of the consequences. Without faith, we cannot please God (Hebrews 11:6). When we drop our shield of faith, we feel like we're not going to get through our difficult situations. Depression and despair become rampant when we focus on what we see, feel, observe, or think in the midst of our adversity. However, the biblical way of approaching our storm is to walk by faith and not by our circumstances, emotions, or thoughts.

This is not just my personal opinion. A relatively new field of social science called "resiliency" explores how people work through and overcome traumatic events. In their findings, researchers have discovered that people respond to traumatic situations in one of two ways: One response is to quit, feel defeated, or experience a major breakdown. The other response is to become resilient.

Resiliency is a condition in which people who are traumatized will actually enlarge the capacity to handle problems. They won't just survive them but will grow because of them. Likewise, the place where our faith grows the most is in the middle of our difficult circumstances. But this can only happen if we don't quit. We must continue to believe that God is going to cause things to work for our good even when everything looks bad around us.

Let's examine three qualities of a resilient faith.

Quality 1: Resilient Faith Controls What It Can

A person with resilient faith is able to exercise control in a stress-filled environment. When studying prisoners of war (POWs) from the Vietnam prison camps, we see this principle at work. The POWs lost a lot of control of their daily existence. They were confined to tiny jail cells, restricted from going outdoors, and had no choice in what they ate. The soldiers who passively accepted losing that much control of their lives tended to think they had lost total control. They were the least likely to survive in prison or recover from the post-traumatic effects at home.

The soldiers who triumphed over their adversity decided to gain some sense of control even in their harsh imprisonment. They put themselves on strenuous exercise regimens, memorized stories, invented new games, took a census of the number of insects in their cell, and created secret signals to communicate with each other. They encouraged one another and reminded themselves that their bodies had been captured but their spirits had not.

As you face your challenging circumstances, remember that by faith your spirit is still alive and well no matter how bad the situation may seem. Don't begin to feel powerless in your circumstance. Real power doesn't come from us anyway. It comes from the God who promised to never leave us or forsake us (Hebrews 13:5). When we can believe that God is with us, we can reject the thoughts of being powerless; we can remember that God has the ability to transform our situation in the blink of an eye.

Faith believes that with God, we are never helpless victims. We see this faith in the life of Joseph (Genesis chapters 37-50). God gave Joseph a dream and, because of that dream, he was sold into slavery, slandered, and locked up in jail. But the Bible says that the Lord stayed with Joseph throughout his adversity, and Joseph never stopped believing that God had a plan for him. He remained resilient in his faith and took control of the adverse situation by working for his master and the prison guard with excellence.

Even though the dream God gave Joseph seemed all but dead, he applied himself diligently to the task at hand. Even though he was a slave, he worked hard to please both God and his master. Joseph became the CEO of each project assigned to him, even in jail. Instead of quitting, he deepened his faith, took control of his circumstances, and became the most powerful and effective leader of his time in all of Egypt.

How do you eat an elephant? One bite at a time. So stop trying to tackle insurmountable problems all at once. Just do what you can little by little and trust God with the rest.

For example, when you can't pay the thousands of dollars you owe on your credit cards, you might be tempted to just walk away from the debt and let the late payments build up. But another option is to make small payments on time and begin to see the total debt decrease. You have done what you could and made progress toward the goal.

Don't let any situation cripple or immobilize you. Instead, practice a resilient faith that obeys God in small areas until you see breakthrough in every area.

QUALITY 2: RESILIENT FAITH DOES NOT QUIT

Quitting oppresses the nature of resilient faith. What if Joseph had a passive spirit and gave up on the vision from the Lord? He would have died a slave. Whatever you are going through or facing right now, don't let it cause you to die a slave so that you never become the ruler that God intended you to be.

It's the adversity in our lives that God uses to prepare us for our destiny. This is why James chapter 1 instructs us to consider it joy when we face trials (v. 2). He also says that these trials are testing our faith and our faith develops perseverance (v. 3). All of this perseverance leads us to become complete. Complete doesn't mean Christ is finished with us. It means that we don't lack anything we need to become finished (v.4). We just need to learn how to use what we have in more effective ways.

I have grown tremendously and am a better woman as a result of each of my trials. Now God is able to use me in new and living ways such as writing this book. I know that God will use this work to minister to hurting men and women like you; Because of this, I am so grateful that God has blessed me with the trials of the death of my parents and husband as well as the difficult childhood years with an alcoholic/abusive father. No, I would not choose to go through these ordeals, but going through them have made me who I am in Christ today.

I have also learned that what Romans 8:28 says is true: "We know that in all things God works for the good of those who love him." This means that God is working all things good and bad for our good. Yes, it's easier to walk out on a marriage than to break down the walls separating us from our spouse. It's certainly easier to quit on pursuing our dreams than to work hard to see them come to pass. Quitting seems like such a sweet relief to our problems that when life doesn't turn out the way we want or believed it would, many of us just give up.

We experience real growth and blessings, though, when we exert control where we can rather than give up. It happens when we decide to be wholly faithful in a situation that we don't like or can't understand.

Resilient faith requires controlling what we can in our traumatic situations and choosing not to quit.

QUALITY 3: RESILIENT FAITH DISCOVERS PURPOSE IN THE STORM

We often find meaning in simple places. Perhaps in a child's laughter or the flight pattern of a bird. It doesn't really matter where we are, it just matters that we look for God to reveal the purpose of our life in our storm.

Joseph found meaning in the simplicity of helping others while he was in jail. Joseph helped two cellmates, a baker and a butler, who came to him with their troubling dreams. It would have been so easy for Joseph to isolate himself in a corner and focus only on his own disappointments, but he focused on others around him.

When life doesn't turn out the way we plan, we often forget that people around us are facing disappointment too. If we're not careful, we begin to believe that we are the only ones who are hurting. Our world, then, becomes so focused on ourselves that our pain is the only thing we notice. This self-focus causes death of the heart and the loss of meaning and purpose for our lives.

The fact is, when we are preoccupied with ourselves, we express self-defeating thoughts, which produces loneliness and depression. Ask yourself if, during stormy periods of your life, you have expressed genuine concern for others when you have had nothing to gain. Do you continuously complain to others about those who have hurt you? If you answered yes to the latter, then you are preoccupied with your own self. While in prison, Joseph could have easily been self-focused, too, but he realized he wasn't the only one for whom life didn't turn out as planned. He turned his attention to the plight of his cellmates; he lived as Jesus lived by showing sincere concern for them.

It was no accident that Joseph spent years as a slave and then a prisoner. These trials sharpened his resiliency and made him ready to be exalted to a prominent position where he could be used by God.

Joseph would have never been ready for such favor by God before his imprisonment. At that time, Joseph was the favorite child of his father. He could not enter into community with his brothers because they didn't want to accept his favored position. Even with the sibling issues, life was easy for Joseph at home. As a slave, though, Joseph learned how to work hard, increase in integrity, and live in servanthood. As a prisoner, he developed compassion for others and understood that God was enough even when everything else was lost. He finally became a man God could use.

I didn't know much about the life of Joseph at the time, but I do remember writing about the purpose of trials for my college entrance essay. The prompt said, "Write about the person who has influenced your life the most." I could have written about Jesus; at seventeen years old, he impacted my life in profound ways. Or I could have written about my amazing mother, who raised us with much love and compassion despite being verbally and physically abused by my father. I thought about choosing my brother, who was like a father and always there for me. But I didn't choose any of these wonderful people. Instead, I chose to write about the person who caused me the most pain. I chose to write about my emotionally absent, physically abusive, verbally assaultive, drunken father.

Why? Well, if my father would have paid the bills instead of drinking his money away, I would have never experienced poverty and living on government assistance. If my father had treated my mother with decency and respect, I would have never demanded to have someone treat me that way as an adult. If my father did not live as an alcoholic, I would not have made choices to live free of alcohol and drugs in my own life. If my father had shown me love, care, and compassion, I would not have learned to lean on Jesus Christ. If my father had never beat my mother or stabbed her with a knife, I would not have cried out to God as my Savior for help.

Now, because of my father, I have compassion for those who are hurting. For example, I understand women who are victims of domestic abuse much better than others do. I value the gifts and the blessings that the Lord has provided to me because I know what it is to be poor. Without my alcoholic father, I would not have a passion to see others live a victorious life nor challenge them to believe the promises of God. Not only is my life more mature and complete because of him, the thousands of lives that God has allowed me to touch are more mature and complete as well.

It's absolutely true that resilient faith best expresses itself when life doesn't turn out the way we had planned. For everyone, sooner or later, the storm strikes—in our marriage, family, work, ministry, finances, or health. It's in the act of controlling what we can and persevering in the storm through a resilient faith that we discover what lies inside of us.

CHAPTER 9

PROTECTION FROM LOSING YOUR MIND
(Helmet of Salvation)

Pain of mind is worse than pain of body.
~ Latin Proverb

On June 16, 2011, the leaders of our church held a meeting at my home. It was customary during these meetings for all of us to leave our children, including my two sons, with a babysitter at another house. The particular meeting was only supposed to last one and a half hours. However, as church meetings go, we went over by almost an hour. As we were trying to wrap up the final stages of the meeting, the phone rang. One of the leaders reached for the handset.

"Hello?" He didn't have to say a thing. Somehow, we all knew it was the babysitter.

"Oh no, what happened?" One of the mothers demanded. "Tell me. Who is hurt?"

"It's Goobie," He said. "He fell out of a window."

"No. No. No. My Goobie, my precious Joshua, fell out of a window! This can't be happening." I left everyone at my house and raced to the babysitter only a three-minute drive away.

During those three minutes, I prayed so fervently, "Lord, no. Please don't let anything happen to my Goobie. Lord, I can't take another loss. I just lost my husband two years ago and now this. Oh Lord, I need you to protect, keep, and heal my son." Feelings from despair to hope collided in my head.

When I approached the house, I heard the Lord speak ever so gently, "Everything is going to be okay." I ran inside to find my son's limp body in the arms of the babysitter. "What happened?" I yelled, grabbing my son and placing him into my own arms.

"Mommy." My eight-year old cried, "No. I don't want Goobie to die. Mommy please don't let Goobie die." He had suffered enough loss when his dad died. He certainly couldn't bear the thought of seeing his little brother die, too. I could not console him now. I left him crying on my shoulder.

"Goobie, wake up, talk to Mommy. Mommy is here. Say something." His eyes were closed, his body lifeless, but he could moan.

"Goobie, talk to Mommy please. Can you touch where it hurts? Say something."

Just then, several of the parents of the other children arrived.

"What happened!" screamed the owner. "What happened!"

"I don't know," the sitter said. "He fell out of the window and onto the driveway. Next thing I hear is 'Don't move him. Call the ambulance, quickly.'"

I placed my Goobie on the couch and began to pray.

"Goobie broke my window!" Shouted a two-year old, jumping up and down on the couch. "Goobie broke my window!"

Within minutes, the paramedics arrived. They cut his shirt and began to work on my little, moaning, and lifeless child. The EMT called on the radio, "We have a five year-old male who fell twenty feet from a second story window . . ."

"We have to rush him to the hospital," he said. In the ambulance, I found out they were transporting him to a Pediatric Trauma Unit twenty minutes away.

"This can't be good." I thought.

After, the examinations, x-rays, and CT scans, they told me that Joshua suffered a severe fracture to his skull in two locations, among other injuries.

"The next few days are critical," the neurosurgeon said. "We have to watch him very closely for brain swelling and changes in his behavior to determine if we need to operate. He will survive, but he will not be able to play sports, ride bikes, or climb a play structure for at least one year."

I knew our brains were important, but I never realized how fragile they truly are. My son's face and head swelled to astronomical sizes and unconventional proportions. He fought hard to be freed from the restraints of a totally restrictive neck brace. He forgot everything that happened in relation to the accident. I cried over all of that, but through this adversity and the five days in the Pediatric Intensive Care Unit, I saw God's loving angels wrap their arms around my son and keep him safe.

In the middle of this trial, God also began to speak to me about the importance of protecting our brain and our mind. After the accident, I was preparing to teach a Bible study class and ran across the following article in the Lansing

State Journal dated June 23, 2009 about a 36 year-old man who had a skateboarding accident:

> It was a death that could have been avoided, officials said. Paul Maxim, who was not wearing a helmet, suffered a skull fracture and other head injuries in an accident June 18 at Ranney Skate Park near Frandor. He died Saturday. A simple helmet would have saved his life,' said Lansing fire public information officer Steve Mazurek.1

Now consider this article that appeared in the *Manchester Evening News* on July 4, 2008:

> Savannah Haworth, 11, was knocked unconscious after falling into the path of the car. The wheels went over her arm and top of her helmet but she escaped with a swollen elbow and bruising to her face. Her parents say she would have been killed without the helmet and are now urging all cyclists to wear them.
>
> Savannah, from Helmshore, in Rossendale, showed the shattered remains of the helmet to fellow pupils at her primary school in an assembly to warn of the dangers of not wearing one.2

In one case, skateboarding without a helmet caused death; and in the other case, wearing a helmet saved a girl's life, even after being run over by a car! In a similar way, the helmet of salvation can save us from spiritual death regardless of the circumstance. It's another piece of spiritual armor that should not be underestimated (see Ephesians 6).

Our mind is the battlefield of the enemy. It is the place where we formulate our beliefs and values that ultimately govern our thoughts and actions. In fact, most of our struggles during adversity are not with any situation or circumstance, but with the thoughts that rage in our minds.

We struggle with thoughts of suicide, low self-worth, hopelessness, despair, anger, hate, malicious acts of violence, lust, indecency, etc. Thoughts like these racing through our minds in the middle of trying circumstances can make us feel like we are going to "lose our minds." These thoughts are tactics of the enemy; they take our minds captive and prevent us from experiencing victory during trials. It shouldn't surprise us, though. The devil doesn't really have any new tactics; they're the same since the days of Adam and Eve.

Our challenge is to take back the captivity of our thoughts from the enemy and make them captive and obedient to Christ (2 Corinthians 10:5). The helmet of salvation will help us do this. To understand how to use this piece of armor, let's take a look at Satan's tactics in the Garden of Eden.

Remember that Satan is a master of deception. He appeared in the Garden as a serpent and his lies caused Eve to begin to question the very words of God. She became temporarily confused, ate the fruit that God told her not to eat, and gave it to her husband who ate it as well. After they both disobeyed God, their eyes were opened to the effects of their disobedience (their sin); and as a consequence, they lost their perfect living arrangements (Genesis 2-3).

In Genesis 3:13, Eve explains her actions: "The serpent deceived me, and I ate."

Miriam Webster defines "deceive" as "to cause to accept as true or valid what is false or invalid."[3] Since this first lie with Eve, Satan continues to work extremely hard to get believers to accept his lies as truth. Why? Because if we accept his lies as truth, we will base our actions on his lies and not on God's truth.

One of Satan's lies has to do with our salvation. In the middle of a crisis, especially one caused by our own mistakes, we often begin to question if we are really saved. However, once we've given our life to Jesus Christ, we can be assured of the hope that when we die, we will enter heaven and continue our eternal relationship with Jesus Christ (1 Thessalonians 5:8).

Even with this knowledge, during a trying time of life, we still tend to ask God, "Am I really saved?" Sometimes people ask this about us, too. Many of the attacks against me, for instance, surround the fact that I am a Christian. "Well," they say, "if you were a 'real' Christian, you would not have done or said . . . . "

The idea that all Christians are perfect is a deception and a myth. The truth is that all Christians make mistakes. We are not perfect; *we are being perfected*. God is still working some things out of us. We won't be finished until we see Jesus. *So do not allow a mistake that you made to be used as a reason to doubt your salvation.*

When Satan tries this trick, just remind him that you were not saved by anything you did or didn't do—you were saved by the blood of Jesus. "For it is by grace you have been saved, through faith . . . not by works, so that no one can boast" (Ephesians 2:8-9). Our salvation is secure because we cannot earn it. It is a free gift lavished on us by the love of God through the death of his son, Jesus Christ. And just in case you begin to feel a little guilty about something you did that was wrong, remind yourself of God's truth: "There is now no condemnation for those who are in Christ Jesus" (Romans 8:1).

Satan does not stop at attacking the hope of our salvation. He also throws all kinds of evil and lewd thoughts into our minds. He does so with the hope that we will entertain these thoughts and begin to commit sins. He bombards us with lies, doubts, and subliminal messages about our faith, hoping that we will change our convictions and values and no longer trust in God. Through these mental attacks, he tries to get us utterly discouraged. And when I, as a Christian, say, "Oh, no. Satan could never deceive me," I am reminded of what Paul wrote: "I am afraid that just as Eve was deceived by the serpent's cunning, your minds may somehow be led astray from your sincere and pure devotion to Christ" (2 Corinthians 11:3). We can never take off our helmet lest our minds be somehow led astray.

Satan is so crafty that he will even use the word of God to twist what we know to be true. He used this tactic on Jesus in Matthew chapter 4 when he tried to confuse Jesus about what God "really said" concerning his immortality. If Jesus believed Satan, he would have fallen to his death three years before his appointed time, or at least broke most of his bones, and the prophecy about the coming Messiah would not have been fulfilled. The purpose of Jesus' life would have been null and void.

When Satan tries to confuse us, we often really want what he is offering. We really want to believe that it's okay to have the mansion on a hill, the other woman, the corner office. After all, doesn't God really desire to bless us with benefits and pleasures? Doesn't God want us to get out of this situation by any means necessary?

Satan wants us to believe that we can hang on to God and also have what we want, when we want, how we want it. "After all the pain we've been through, don't we deserve something positive or fun or satisfying in our lives?"

Satan replies, "Absolutely." He makes us think that compromise of our values and convictions to obtain this pleasure is healthy. In marriage, for example, we tell people that compromise works. In a human relationship of equal partners, yes, compromise works. However, in a relationship with a holy God, compromise with him on his word cannot and does not work on any level. Partial obedience to God is full disobedience.

When we are confused, it's okay to take a break and say, "Lord, I really need to figure out what you say about this before I make any moves." Don't feel worried, depressed, or hopeless. Just take a step back and ask God to help sort out the feelings. When I desire something and I'm not sure if it's God's will or not, I ask, "Lord, help me to determine if I want this because you want it for me or because I want it for me."

God is so faithful; he will let us know the desires of our heart even when we're not sure where they came from. God wants us to know his will for our lives. He tells us that when we seek his will, desire, and purpose for our lives, we will find it in him when we search for him with all our hearts (Jeremiah 29:12-14).

The next question, then, is how do we protect our minds? How do we actually put on and use the "helmet of salvation"? The first thing we must realize is that we have victory over Satanic attacks because we have been given the mind of Christ (1 Corinthians 2:16). The challenge for us during trying circumstances is to choose to have the mind of Christ and not let the world infiltrate our minds.

To meet this challenge, there are two keys to obtaining victory over deceiving thoughts. The first key, we will discuss in this chapter and the second we will discuss in the next chapter.

KEY 1: WATCH WHAT ENTERS OUR MIND

The first key is to watch what enters our mind. Satan uses powerful, subliminal messages to challenge our personal beliefs and absolute truths. Society for example, teaches that truth is subjective, not absolute. But real truth does not change no matter the circumstance.

Real truth is that 2 + 2 = 4. No matter how much we may believe that it equals 8, especially in relation to our bank accounts, nothing we do will change the fact that the sum of 2 + 2 always equals 4. However, society doesn't operate in this absolute value system. It believes that the boundary lines can be moved, morality is subject to popular opinion, and integrity means not being caught. "2 + 2 does not always equal 4," they say.

We see this principle clearly with the issue of sex on television. I remember when *I Love Lucy* was on in the 1950s. Well, actually, I remember watching the reruns in the 90s because I wasn't born yet to see the original airings. Nevertheless, Lucy and Ricky slept in separate, twin beds— that was family television. Now, in 2011, people have sex on television in all kinds of positions and with all kinds of people, even people outside of marriage. Advertisers also believe that in order to sell products, they have to promote sex. Do women really need to jump on a man and try to take his clothes off because of the shampoo and body wash he is using? Could the enemy be desensitizing our ability to know what truth truly is?

The truth is that using the "right" shampoo and body wash is not going to bring dozens of women into a man's bedroom. I believe most people realize that, but the images move our lustful desires enough that we decide to buy the product based on our sinful desires and emotions. It's easy to see why we, as American Christians, can be moved on moral issues so easily, especially in the last sixty years as moral decline has become so prevalent in mass media. The solution is to protect our minds.

Remember that our mind is a battlefield where we actively engage the enemy. When we get lazy and allow tempting messages to enter, we give ammunition to our opponent. It's like falling asleep on the front lines in Afghanistan during an attack. Falling asleep is what Americans do every day. We turn off the pressures of our families, our health, our jobs, our finances, and every area of life by turning on the television so that we can "veg" out and not think about anything remotely difficult.

While escaping, we allow Satan to send us a myriad of negative, self-defeating messages that are contrary to the promises God has for our lives. As we watch the lavish lives of *Real Housewives*, for instance, we get dissatisfied with what "little" we have in our own lives. We let soap operas tell us how to look for a better spouse when we're not satisfied with our own. We let reality television cause us to think that the drama is natural and an absence of drama in our lives is unnatural. We see sex outside of marriage as the norm but celibacy as weird and abnormal.

Don't get me wrong. Television can be an effective vehicle to promote positive programs that reinforce the truth of God's word. Our ministry airs a nationwide television program to help combat the lies and spread the truth of God's word. So I do believe that television with spiritually healthy programming can be a valuable use of time. I wish more people used television in this way.

How do you use television? During the next week, pay attention to the programs you watch and the commercials that come on during the show. Ask yourself, "Is this in line with God's word or is it working against it?" Ask yourself, "While I'm watching this show, is it helping me to deal with my crisis or is it making me feel worse about my current situation?" The answers to these questions will help you make wiser choices about what to watch on television and in the theater.

I made a decision about fifteen years ago to no longer watch R-rated movies. I'm sure some fine-quality stories have been crafted into age-restricted films, but I don't see the benefit in my life to watching them. Nudity and sex scenes don't help me to live as a single, saved, and celibate woman of God. In fact, I find it quite difficult to get rid of those visual images after they enter my mind. Even movie previews instill unwanted images into my thoughts. In fact, I'm still fighting against images I saw on the big screen years ago.

It's not only what we see that tempts and taunts us, it's also what we hear. The language in these movies can be extremely foul. I have, unfortunately, struggled in the past with my own colorful vocabulary, especially when I need to get my point across. Listening to others speak certain words subconsciously causes those words to occasionally come out of my mouth. Even as a pastor, I have to stop and correct myself after hearing some of the words that slip out.

Music is another powerful tool of the enemy because its enchanting rhythms often allow deceiving thoughts to slip into the lyrics without us realizing it. I can't tell you how many popular songs I sang by heart in high school and college. When I listen to these songs today, I think, "Wow. I had no idea they were talking about that." Is it any wonder that I struggled so much with sex outside of marriage during those days?

Let's also not forget about the novels we read. The pictures that well-written sex scenes or murder mysteries conjure up in our head can be just as dangerous as watching them on TV. Our mind cannot separate real pictures from those designed by talented authors. Quite often, those pictures linger in our mind and can deceive us as well. The same is true for looking at advertisements and photographs in popular magazines.

Deception is the key of the world. The key of God in fighting off the enemy's tactics within our minds is to place a shield of protection around it. This shield is the helmet of salvation and wearing it allows God to cover us from the devil's tricky deceptions. It provides protection and helps us to keep from "losing our mind."

The second key to overcoming deceiving thoughts is to fill our helmets with God's words, not Satan's, Let's move onward, then, and learn how to hear and use the powerful words of God.

CHAPTER 10

STICKS AND STONES
BREAK BONES, BUT
THE WORD HEALS
(Sword of the Spirit)

So is my word that goes out from my mouth;
It will not return to me empty, but will accomplish what I desire an
achieve the purpose for which I sent it.

~ Isaiah 55:1

The breastplate of righteousness, helmet of salvation, and belt of truth defend us against the attacks of the enemy. But there are two offensive weapons that help us to launch our own attacks. The first one we looked at in chapter 4 is prayer. The other is the word of God. Nothing will transform us from breakdown to breakthrough like prayer and the word of God.

Paul describes God's word as "the sword of the Spirit" because God's word is sharp and it penetrates the spirit. It judges our mind, thoughts, and attitudes (Hebrews 4:12). This sword is not like our nation's weapons that boasts of guns, tanks, bombs, and fighter jets. No. The word of God has divine power that is able to tear down strongholds in our minds, families, bodies, finances, and more (2 Corinthians 10:4).

It's so powerful that it lasts forever.

It has the ability to alter the very course of our destiny.

It has the power to divinely accomplish exactly what it was purposed to do in exactly the right time (Isaiah 55:11).

It has the power to break you out of your downtrodden state and transform you into a victorious vessel for Jesus Christ.

Simply put, the word of God has power!

Most of us don't realize that we are soldiers fighting hand-to-hand combat in the middle of a very real war. We know, for example, there is a war going on in the Middle East; but unless we have a loved one in the battle, we're not so concerned about it. However, if we were soldiers in the war, we wouldn't be able to forget, on a daily basis, that the war is real. Likewise, we must open our eyes to our spiritual foe and see the reality of the war. It is time to pull out our sword.

To be effective, though, the sword must come in close contact with the enemy. Imagine an Olympic fencing match. The opponents don't joust far apart from each other. Their swords can't wield any power at that distance. With intensity, purpose, and direct contact, the fencers use their swords to attack and defend until victory is won. Likewise, the more directly the word of God is used as a weapon to defend and attack the lies of the enemy in strategic moments, the more powerful its effects.

Speaking the word of God is effective when the mind struggles with the enemy's deceptions or when he attacks what is most personal to us—friends, family, health, or finances. It works particularly well when we feel completely defeated or frustrated.

This is why it's so important to wake up early in the morning and spend time with God. As we read through the Bible systematically, God will cause a Scripture to stand out for us. We might realize that this word has special meaning for our lives, but we're not exactly sure what it could be. Then, as we go through the day, a new problem, or a part of the old problem, confronts us. At that moment, we remember that God provided a word for us earlier that morning. That word is our sword—a weapon intended to strengthen and encourage us during this fight (the seven keys later in this chapter explain exactly how to use the word in these situations).

As you practice wielding the sword of the spirit, you will discover that God's word is designed to support you in the specific issue you are dealing with. Second Corinthians 10:13 says that the word is mighty for pulling down strongholds. Strongholds are areas of your life that you've tried to have victory over but still seem to struggle with. They just won't let go. No matter how hard you try to stop doing the sin, for instance, you just can't stop. It has a hold on you so strong, you can't even run away because it's stronger than you.

These strongholds may be drugs, alcohol, bad relationships, unforgiveness, overspending, overeating, fear, etc. They are designed by the enemy to make sure we're held captive by them. We continue to struggle with these strongholds because we're all tied up, like a prisoner, and feel helpless to fix or alleviate our problem. But no matter what the issue is, we can always fight back with God's word. Jeremiah

23:29 describes God's word like fire and a hammer that can shatter a solid rock into pieces. There is no stronghold that God's word is not able to tear down in your life.

Not only is the word of God *powerful* enough to tear down strongholds, it's also *proven*. God's word has lasted since the beginning of time. Isaiah 40:8 says that God's word lasts forever. No matter what happened to the earth over the centuries, the word of God has stood the test of time.

The word of God is *practical*, too. It will provide guidance and direction for you in the midst of your adversity. Psalms 119:105 says that God's word will provide light to our feet and our path. That means that his word will illuminate the path that God desires us to take while traveling through the darkness. His word helps to make decisions clear and provides understanding in the midst of confusion. Real victory can only be found in the word of God. *We have no choice but to use this weapon.*

Now that I have told you why the word of God is the most powerful weapon we have, it is time to teach you how to use it. After all, what good is a destroyer jet in the hands of a soldier who doesn't know how to fly a plane? We can know that God's word has power; but without knowing how to use his word, we are just as defenseless as if we had no weapons at all.

Unfortunately, we can't just pick up a Bible, hold it up in front of our face, and hope that the enemy will leave us alone, like in *The Exorcist* movies. We must know how to use the sword in order to live victorious and come out of our turbulent situations. These seven keys will help us do that:

KEY 1: PRAY THE WORD

In Acts 4, Peter and John were on trial before the religious leaders. When they were finally released, they joined together with other believers to pray. In the New International Version, there's a note after verses 25-26 that points to Psalm 2:1-2 as a reference for their prayer. Peter, John, and the others prayed out loud the exact words of Psalm 2:1-2. Then they asked God to give them power and boldness. Acts 4:31 says that after they prayed, power filled the room and it started to shake. Their prayers were answered; the Spirit of God filled the people empowering them to courageously speak God's word.

The first church knew they were going to face opposition, so they prepared for the battle by praying the word. As they prayed the word, God began to move in their hearts so that they were able to preach the word of God boldly. They were able to speak in public what they had prayed in private. So don't be afraid to take a passage of Scripture and pray it. When we pray God's word with the right heart and right motive, God moves.

KEY 2: PREACH THE WORD

This is where you might say, "That will work for you, Pastor Sheyna, because you're a preacher, but what about those of us who don't feel that kind of call on our lives?" The reality is that preaching the word is not just for ordained ministers or those who feel called to preach. To preach means to proclaim the word. Pulpits don't stand only in front of a church on Sunday mornings. Pulpits stand in every believer's office, car, living room, and favorite restaurant.

There's nothing the enemy hates more in the middle of our adversity than to hear us proclaim the word to someone else. You might think you have to wait until the trial ends to tell someone else how great is our God. But that's another lie. The word of God operating in your life becomes your testimony. And keep in mind that a testimony is given in the courtroom while on trial, not after it's all over.

In Acts 4, Peter and John faithfully proclaimed the word of God in the temple in the midst of persecutions and imprisonments of Christians. God is calling us to do the same. Don't wait until your circumstance gets better. Right now, in the middle of your trial, tell someone about how good and faithful God has been.

Proclaiming the word, removes fear and doubt and releases confidence in God. It injects a supernatural infusion of faith that strengthens us to face the mini trials of each day. If we have no one to preach to, we can encourage ourselves by preaching the word to ourselves. Many days, I have to stand in front of the mirror and boldly proclaim what God's word says to me. I especially like to remind myself of the promises of God. By the time I've finished preaching to myself, I'm ready for any challenges the day brings.

KEY 3: SING THE WORD

Praying and preaching bring about powerful spiritual results. And so does singing. In Acts 16, Paul released a demonic spirit from a young slave girl. Instead of receiving thanks, he and a fellow disciple named Silas were attacked by the crowd, stripped, beaten, and placed in prison. I can only imagine the feelings of despair, hopelessness, and anger that I would have felt in that situation. However, the Bible says that around midnight, Paul and Silas were praying and singing hymns to God—hymns of Scripture.

As a child, I learned songs with Scripture in the lyrics. Those Scriptures have stayed with me my entire life and I rely on them during difficult times. When I feel alone, for example, I listen to Israel Houghton sing "I Am a Friend of God." When I need to be reminded of the power of God, I sing Chris Tomlin's "How Great Is Our God." When I'm confused, I'm reminded that God has a plan for me by singing Martha Munizzi's "I Know the Plans" based on Jeremiah 29:11.

Don't worry about whether you can sing or not. Just pretend you're in the shower and sing for yourself and for God. When you're going through a challenging time, the word of God combined with the beat of the music can lift your soul, mind, body, and spirit.

I used this key a lot when I was trying to remain celibate. At the age of nineteen, I decided that I needed to rid my mind of all secular lyrics, so I sold all of my CDs and only listened to gospel music. Whenever I was tempted to have a lustful thought or it got too hot and heavy with my boyfriend, I began to sing songs with Scripture. I remember singing, "Victory Is Mine" while reminding myself of 1 Corinthians 15:57, which says that I have victory in Jesus.

It's strange how singing Scripture confuses the enemy in the middle of a fight. Satan wants us to be depressed and stressed out, but singing God's word lifts our spirit. We can be going through one of the most difficult times in our lives; and yet, we have joy because we are singing the promises of God into the atmosphere.

The Bible says that as Paul and Silas were singing, a violent earthquake occurred. Their chains broke loose and everyone in the jail cell got freed. Something happens when we lift our voices in song. It not only brings deliverance for us but for those in our homes and communities who hear us singing the very words of God.

KEY 4A: READ THE WORD

You can't use a weapon that you're not familiar with. In other words, the more you're familiar with God's word, the more you will be able to use the word of God in any situation. Don't worry if you're not a Bible scholar. A simple reading plan of fifteen minutes of Scripture each day is a great way to start. You can begin by reading one Psalm, one chapter of Proverbs, and one chapter of John each day. The Proverbs are divided into 31 chapters, which correspond to a 31-day month. So if today is the 15th of the month, start with chapter 15 of Psalms and Proverbs and chapter 1 of the book of John.

If you want to read more, pick an Old Testament book and a New Testament book and read one chapter of each a day. You might also want to find a study plan for reading through the Bible in a year or pick up a book of devotions. I encourage you, though, to choose a devotional book that has ample Scriptures and questions to help you reflect on what you read. Make sure you're spending time reading God's word and not just the author's word.

KEY 4B: READ THE WORD ALOUD

Our faith is increased when we hear the word. Romans 10:17 in the KJV says, "Faith cometh by hearing and hearing by the word of God." This means we can increase our faith the more we hear God's word. Reading the word aloud allows us to hear words in Scripture that we may not have heard before. It releases the power of God in the atmosphere and causes the enemy to tremble with fear.

KEY 5: MEDITATE ON THE WORD

Another way to fight the enemy with the sword of the Spirit is to meditate on the word. Meditating on the word is reading the word with the goal of applying it to your life. In other words, it is looking at the word and discovering what God wants us to DO with it. Joshua 1:8 says, "Do not let this Book of the Law depart from your mouth; meditate on it day and night, so that you may be careful *to do everything written in it*. Then you will be prosperous and successful" (italics added).

To get a better idea of what God wants us to do with his word, we have to seriously think about it. For instance, pick one Scripture from your reading that God seems to be putting on your heart to apply to your life. As you think about it, ask yourself these six basic questions:

- *Who* is the Scripture speaking to?

- *What* is the Scripture about?

- *When* was it written?

- *Where* is the context of the passage?

- *Why* did God want me to focus on this passage?

- *How* should I apply this to my life?

Meditating on the word releases life-giving power from the text. It allows the Holy Spirit to reveal rich illumination in us and new insight into our situation. It also helps to remind us of the promises God has for us.

KEY 6: PERSONALIZE THE WORD

Put your own name in the word. It really makes the word of God come alive. If you find a passage that really speaks to you, substitute the pronouns with your name. One that I love to recite when faced with adversity is Psalm 91:10-16.

Read this passage below and everywhere you see a blank line insert your name:

[10]No harm will befall _____ no disaster will come near her tent.

[11]For he will command his angels concerning _____ to guard her in all her ways;

[12]They will lift _____ up in their hands, so that she will not strike her foot against a stone.

[13]_____ will tread upon the lion and the cobra; she will trample the great lion and the serpent.

[14]"Because _____ loves me," says the Lord, "I will rescue her; I will protect her, for she acknowledges my name.

[15] _____ will call upon me, and I will answer her; I will be with her in trouble, I will deliver her and honor her.

[16]With long life will I satisfy_____ and show her my salvation."

Personalizing Scripture is an effective way to banish fear, disillusionment, and hopelessness as well as remind ourselves of the promises of God.

KEY 7: MEMORIZE THE WORD

While I use keys 1-6 regularly with powerful results, no other key has so radically transformed my life as memorizing Scripture. Psalm 119:11 says, "I have hidden your word in my heart that I might not sin against you." When I have defeating or discouraging thoughts, I am more tempted to believe them and disobey God. But during these times, I often don't have my Bible to look up a Scripture that I know will help me. I'll remember that I read it that morning and I'll even know which side of the Bible it's on, but I don't quite remember exactly what book or chapter the Scripture is in the word.

The key to keeping the word securely hidden in the heart is to memorize Scripture. Keep a box, book, or Ziploc bag of index cards with God's promises for you. I write Scriptures that God has revealed to me in my journal and then once a week I transfer the Scriptures in my journal to index cards. I keep the index cards with me throughout the week and continue to recite them until I have learned the Scripture. I also write the Scripture down several times to help me memorize it. Once I know the Scripture word for word and can recite it, I place the index card in a small binder. Since I started this exercise about two years ago, I have memorized over two hundred Scriptures.

The value in doing this is not so I can say, "Wow, look at what a Bible scholar I've become." No. The value is that when the enemy tries to attack my mind with negative, defeating thoughts, I can immediately call to mind through the power of the Holy Spirit the memorized Scripture that attacks the very nature of the issue that I'm dealing with.

When I am faced with a financial challenge either for the church or for myself personally, I struggle with believing that God is going to work things out for me. I wrestle constantly, hoping and praying that the children and I will be okay. I go back and forth over whether God can make a way out of what sometimes seems to be a dead end for our ministry.

Whenever I get in this state of mind, I think about God's word. The Holy Spirit often reminds me of 2 Corinthians 9:8, which says, "And God is able to make all grace abound to you, so that in all things at all times, having all that you need, you will abound in every good work." Immediately, my mind is at peace. As soon as I recite that passage, God protects my mind from any other negative thoughts and I am able to move forward in my day with peace and faith.

The Bible tells us that the Holy Spirit will remind us of what God has said to us. The challenge for us is that he will not remind us of something that we have never heard or read.

CHAPTER 11

BREAKDOWN TO BREAKTHROUGH

There is no breakthrough without a break.

~ Pastor Sheyna L. Heard

The journey from breakdown to breakthrough is not an easy one. It requires much work, sacrifice, and tears. However, if you can continue to press through the pain and work through all of the challenges, then you will experience a breakthrough that is designed to take you to another level of maturity and completion in Christ.

Every time I have experienced a breakthrough, I have become a better woman of God. As painful and horrible as I feel while I'm in the situation, it continuously amazes me how God can take my breaking point and use it to transform me.

Since my husband's passing in 2008, for instance, the Lord has given me wisdom as a single mother, to raise my two sons during times of grief, frustration, and disobedience. He has provided me with remarkable creativity to help solve issues with my children that I thought only a man could handle.

God has provided the right words to say on occasions when the children miss their dad and the right disciplinary tools to use when they choose to disobey. He has given me tremendous strength to keep my children involved in activities such as baseball, basketball, flag football, and swimming. I have even had the privilege of coaching my sons in basketball and baseball. I'm happy to report that my boys are excelling both academically and socially.

I have been blessed to become the senior pastor of a fantastic, multi-cultural, non-denominational, outreach-oriented church—Rohi Christian Church in San Jose, California. The church has grown from seventy-five members to over two hundred in only two years. I became the official pastor about two weeks after my husband passed away. The Lord has provided me with wisdom to not only lead my grieving family but a grieving church as well.

The Lord has also allowed me to be the executive director of our nonprofit organization, Rohi Alternative Community Outreach. This organization reaches out to at-risk, gang-involved youth in the San Jose community during late night, high-crime hours. My husband worked with the young men and I worked with the women.

After my husband died, I had big shoes to fill. I had to become the workshop presenter to over sixty troubled, young men each Friday night during the summer. During that time, I learned that I cannot teach young men how to be grown men, but I can love them with the love of Jesus and bring in godly, mature men who can teach them. I have been so blessed by God that, at such a young age, he has allowed me to become a spiritual mother to these young men and women at difficult times in their lives.

I soon realized that I needed to find ways to make money to send my children to college. So the Lord blessed me with starting a real estate investment business. He provided people, resources, and knowledge to start that business while also giving me the ability to work as a licensed realtor.

The health-related deaths of my husband and mother have caused me to focus on my own health and the health of my children. I am now more active and in better shape than I have been in my life. I am cooking more now than I did when my husband was alive. God has blessed me to be able to purchase my first home during this period as well. Now I am working on getting a permanent home for our church, which should be completed by the end of 2011.

I'm grateful to be able to work on a Master's of Divinity from King's Seminary. Through the grace of Christ, I am also able to speak to more men and women in the body of Christ than I ever did before.

I have never felt better about who I am than I do now. I have never felt more confident in Christ, nor has my faith ever been stronger. I am learning to truly walk by faith and not by sight. I'm more comfortable in my own skin and I would not be writing this book if it were not for the tragedies in my life and the power of God that the full armor of God gives me to overcome them. I have greater friendships and feel closer to people than I ever felt before. I am certainly closer to Jesus Christ.

I share all of this with you not to toot my own horn but to let you know that God can truly take our breakdowns and turn them into our breakthroughs. I know that God used the sudden death of my husband to make me stronger, wiser, and better equipped to manage kingdom assignments. He also used it to launch me into ventures that I would have never attempted if it were not for this tragedy. God let me know that there is something amazing inside of me that he could use even when I felt as if I had nothing to offer the world. God truly gave me beauty for my ashes, strength for my pain, joy for my sorrow, and hope for tomorrow.

Before my husband died, I had stopped having my own dreams and goals. They were all tied into whatever he believed that God had for him and the ministry. Only a few months after my husband passed, God reminded me of a vision he had given me eight years earlier. He reminded me of a desire to be a motivational speaker and a vision that I would be speaking to large crowds. He showed me that this dream was still living, active, and relevant for my life. God let me know that the crisis and tragedy of losing my husband simply catapulted me into the destiny and vision of declaring God's glory to the nations. God also gave me new visions and dreams. He gave me creative thoughts and ideas. He restored my passion for life. I loved my life before my husband passed, and I love my life now!

God can truly use our tragedies and turn them into our triumphs. No matter what situation you are facing today, trust God and know that he does work all things out for your good (Romans 8:28). Whatever God is taking you through, he is doing it so that you can become stronger, wiser, and more equipped to carry out his purpose for your life.

Use the tools and the keys learned in this book. Choose to fight through your adversity and conquer the enemy within you. Pray, put on the breastplate of righteousness, the belt of truth, the helmet of salvation. Walk in peace as you carry the sword of the spirit and shield of faith. Put on the full armor of God and break through into a new destiny, a new dimension, and a new level. Allow God to transform your mess into a miracle.

May God's peace, comfort, mercy, grace, forgiveness, strength, power, victory, and love guide you from breakdown to breakthrough!

CHAPTER NOTES

CHAPTER 3

1. James Swanson, *Dictionary of Biblical Languages with Semantic Domains: Greek (New Testament),* electronic ed., (Oak Harbor: Logos Research Systems, 1997), s.v. "katapinō."

2. James Dobson, *Life on the Edge* (Dallas: Word, 1995), 35.

CHAPTER 5

1. Walter Wangerin, *Whole Prayer* (Grand Rapids: Zondervan, 2001), 27.

2. James Patterson and Peter Kim, *The Day America Told the Truth* (Prentice Hall, 1991), 47.

3. Nancy Shulins, "Phony Credentials" Bible.org, (reposting of original article dated 1979), http://bible.org/illustration/phoney-credentials

CHAPTER 9

1. See articles entitled "Paul A. Maxim" and "Deaths" dated June 23, 2009 available to registered, paid users at www.lansingstatejournal.com.

2. Jenny Brookfield and Brian Lashley, "Helmet Saved My Life," *Manchester Evening News,* July 04, 2008, http://menmedia.co.uk/manchestereveningnews/news/s/1056778_helmet_saved_my_life.

3. Merriam-Webster's collegiate dictionary, 11th ed., (Springfield: Merriam-Webster, Inc., 2003), s.v. "deceive."

PERSONAL NOTES